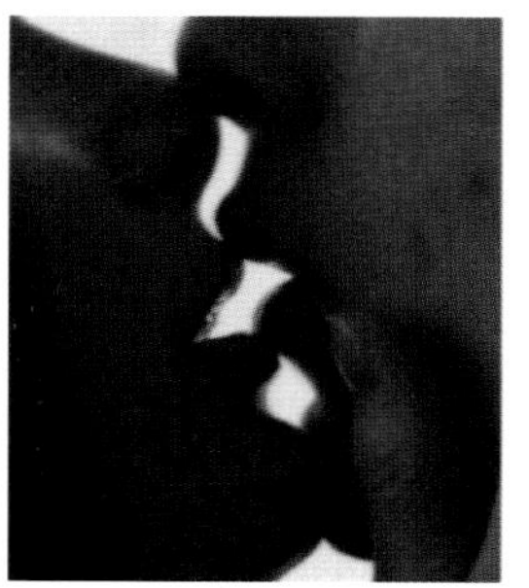

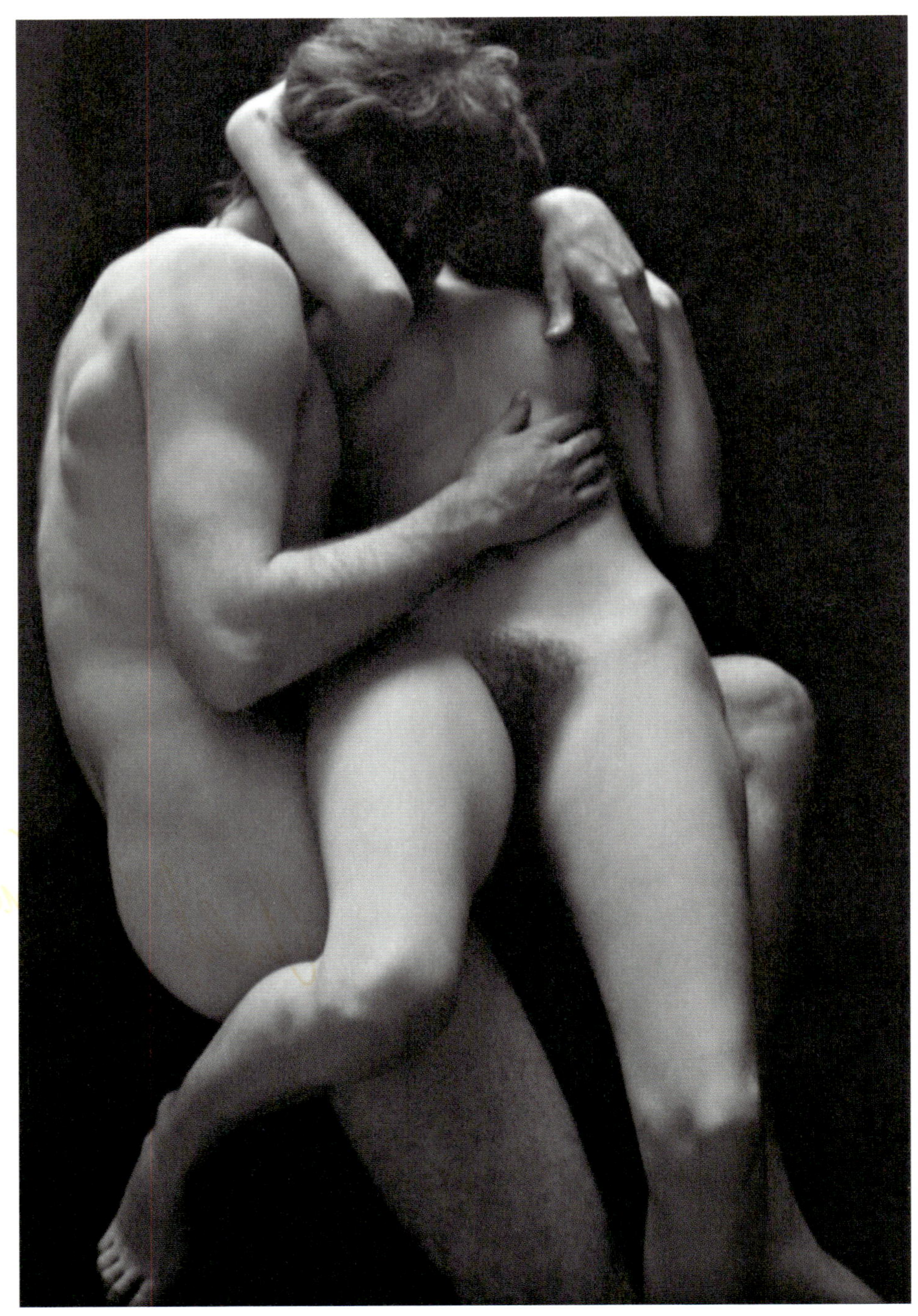

The Erotic Photographs of Arnold Skolnick

Love Song

The Quantuck Lane Press New York

LoveSong by Arnold Skolnick

Printed in Italy
First Edition

Manufacturing by Mondadori Printing, Verona

Digital Imaging by KC Scott
Digital Photographic Prints by Robert Aller
Designed by Arnold Skolnick

Library of Congress Cataloging-in-Publication Data
Skolnick, Arnold.
LoveSong : the erotic photographs of Arnold Skolnick / Arnold Skolnick. — 1st ed.
p. cm.
ISBN 978-1-59372-031-5
1. Photography, Erotic. 2. Skolnick, Arnold. I. Title.
TR676.S57 2008
779'.28—dc22
2007045121

The Quantuck Lane Press
New York
www.quantucklanepress.com

Distributed by W.W. Norton & Company, 500 Fifth Avenue, New York, NY 10110
www.wwnorton.com
W.W. Norton & Company Ltd., Castle House, 75/76 Wells Street, London, WIT 3QT

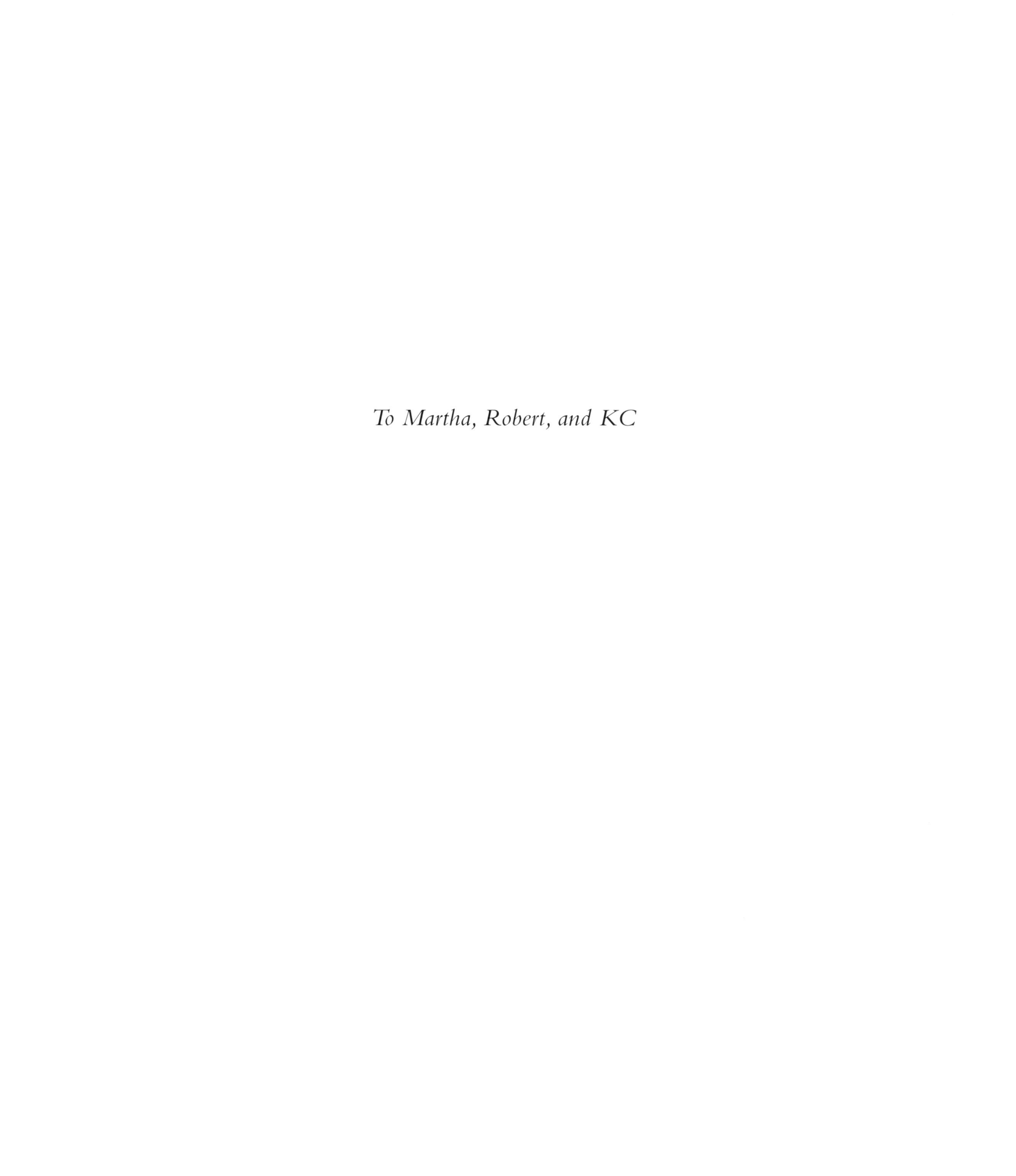

To Martha, Robert, and KC

In 1969 a publisher asked me to make drawings to illustrate a marriage manual. I told him I could do the drawings but I thought photographs would be better. Photography's documentary nature — the immediacy of real people — seemed to me a better way to show a couple's physical connection. I'd seen many photographs of nudes but rarely two bodies together. I wanted to try. The publisher said, "Go ahead."

At the time I was living in New York City. I brought my wife's camera, a clip light, a white canvas, and a large black cloth to a friend's studio in the Village. Then I went to look for a couple. I walked up and down 8th Street — a street known for its hippie clothing and music shops and college students. Not seeing many couples, I asked an attractive young woman if she would be willing to pose. She had no boyfriend but agreed to find a partner — preferably someone who would not actually make love. A partner was found that same day, an agreement was made, and the three of us ascended to the studio.

I was nervous and beginning to have second thoughts. I was not a professional photographer. Could I do it? How would I do it? Though that first shooting was thirty-eight years ago, I remember most of it well — all the decisions I had to make, the problems I had to solve. I had already determined some basics: no props, no particular setting, and no background or foreground — just figures in space and one light source. I always use one light source in my drawings and paintings. There is only one light source in nature. So after having directed the clip light to bounce off the white canvas and laid out the dark cloth covering a mattress on the floor—I was ready.

From the beginning I knew that I didn't want to pose the couple. It seemed a little awkward for me to direct them to embrace or kiss, so I told them to do what they wanted. I would become — through the camera — the voyeur. I waited while they became acquainted and as they began to discover each other, to relax and to touch, a miracle of intimacy unfolded — softness against muscles, curves against angles. They were both brunettes and since I had already set up a dark background, I started to think about lost and found edges, soft or hard shadows. Their faces and bodies emerged out of the darkness, giving them a mysterious and monumental quality. I finally started to shoot. I remember worrying whether the shutter was too loud. I stopped worrying and began composing. I couldn't shoot fast enough to catch all the variations. I was not trying to make art but to capture life. But there was that picture plane to deal with, the forms to balance. It was then that I found the key that would make the pictures work — it was the hand.

The hands. Where were the hands? I started looking for hands. I needed a hand to be in the right place to complete the design, to create the movements, to direct the eye. Hands are also a key to love. How we touch is how we love — hands are crucial.

In my own drawings and paintings I create the forms, the light source, and

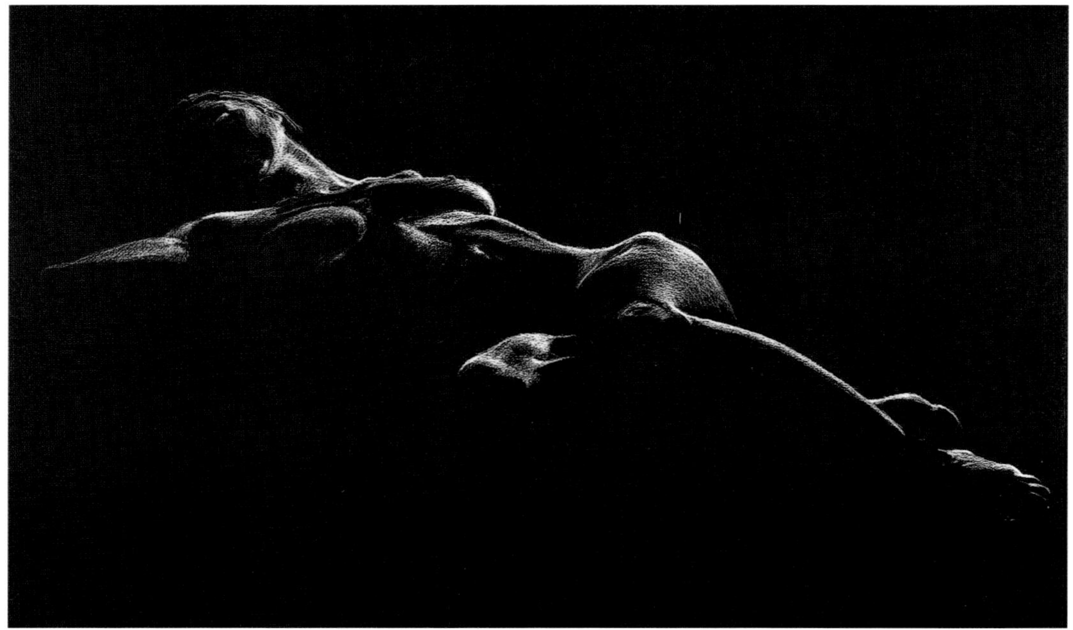

the shadows. I have total control of the composition and of filling the space, which is both a joy and a challenge. I direct the viewer's eye the way I want. In photography the forms are already there — I just have to find them. Change is continuous as the figures stay in position only for a moment, and rarely return. There are also wonderful accidents.

When I checked the contact sheets later, images I thought I had captured were not always there. So many pictures just missed the moment. If only her arm had been higher, if only there had been more light on his back. Matisse would do about thirty drawings and keep just one.

I looked at the contact sheet and saw all the near and complete misses and there was only one, maybe two, with what Cartier-Bresson called "geometry." Everything worked. There was nothing I wanted to change or make better. The Greek definition of beauty is something that is "complete," that can't be changed. The light was ideal, the expressions sublime, the hair falling the right way, the composition faultless and the hand in the right place. It was more than the sum of its parts, much more — it worked. Here were two bodies becoming a universal image. Though photographs capture the literal, it was the ideal that I was after.

The photographs from that first shooting turned out to be some of the best, perhaps because the couple had never met, perhaps because it was a new experience for all of us, or maybe it was just beginner's luck. In any event, I got more than I had been asked to do. The publisher was interested in illustrating sexual positions, and much of what I photographed was romance and tenderness; instead of sex I photographed eroticism. We made a deal and I continued to shoot.

After that first shooting the sessions got a little easier. I put up notices around Greenwich Village advertising for attractive couples and interviewed them looking for a strong connection. Meeting them allowed me to plan the tone of the background — dark or light or gray — to work with the color of their hair. As I continued the shootings, I came up with some interesting setups, producing images that were not necessarily better, only different. Some of the most powerful pictures were created when I dressed in black, stood on the foot of the bed, and shot down on top of the couple while they lay on black fabric. One time I photographed a couple in their bedroom, not a studio, and draped gray paper on the wall behind them. I also experimented with lighting techniques. For one couple I aimed the light higher so it filtered down on top of them, making everything softer, which eliminated any strong shadows. In another setup I placed the light source behind the subjects so they were silhouetted with the light creeping around their bodies.

Of course, much of the power, energy, and tenderness of the photographs came from the emotional connection of the couples. Some were married, some roommates, some had just met. One couple moved like ballet dancers, she the star — he supporting her and directing her, she accommodating him. Another couple seemed to renew their vows — letting body sensations just happen. Once a couple's intimacy became so strong, I shut off the light, left the studio, and returned sometime later. They appreciated it so much they volunteered to do another session. I did not want to photograph them making love. It was the foreplay I wanted to capture. With every couple it was a different experience. Only once did I have to pose them. I asked one couple to come back for a color session. As they entered the studio I heard her say, "Don't touch me." They had had a fight on the way. It took me a while to get them to relax. Posing each picture gave me quite a different look. It was easier in terms of composition, but what the photographs gained aesthetically, they lacked in passion.

In the late sixties people were jailed not for depicting acts of love, but for sending them through the mail. Ralph Ginzburg, the publisher of *Eros* magazine, was hounded through the courts and jailed; the publisher of *The Picture Book of Sexual Love* was jailed for a week in Chicago by Mayor Richard Daley. Spiro Agnew, the governor of Maryland, called and threatened everyone at the publisher's office. The publisher stopped all future projects, including the second volume of the book that I was working on. Some of my pictures appeared in *Psychology Today* and *Sexology* magazine and a number appeared in a book entitled *The Nude in Photography.* In 1973, the Neikrug Gallery in New York City invited me to show many of these photographs in an annual exhibition titled "Rated X." In his review Howard Kissel wrote:

> *From an aesthetic point of view some of the most impressive photos in the exhibition are by Arnold Skolnick which give the forms of two people making love the grandeur and power of sculpture (one is, of course, reminded of Rodin). What is interesting is that the faces are largely shadowed and the emotional impact comes almost entirely from the anonymous bodies. The contrast of the bodies against a dark background provides some drama; the rest comes from the undulating lines of the bodies interacting and the clarity with which tense and moving muscles have been articulated. Again the attitude on the part of both artist and subject is beyond psychological rationale — the most intimate act is simply a pretext for a powerful aesthetic experience.*

After the review appeared, *Playboy* magazine asked me to send a portfolio of pictures for a feature. The editor ultimately changed his mind and returned the photographs damaged. So I had good reasons to file them away and move on. But I didn't forget them. Now, after more than thirty years, having reached my seventieth birthday and having recovered from a recent health crisis, I took the advice of friends to "do something" with them. Robert Aller, a fine art photographer, scanned some images to a disc and made some new prints. When Jim Mairs, publisher of The Quantuck Lane Press, saw some of the images, he decided to publish them. He and I think these images are some of the best.

Love Song

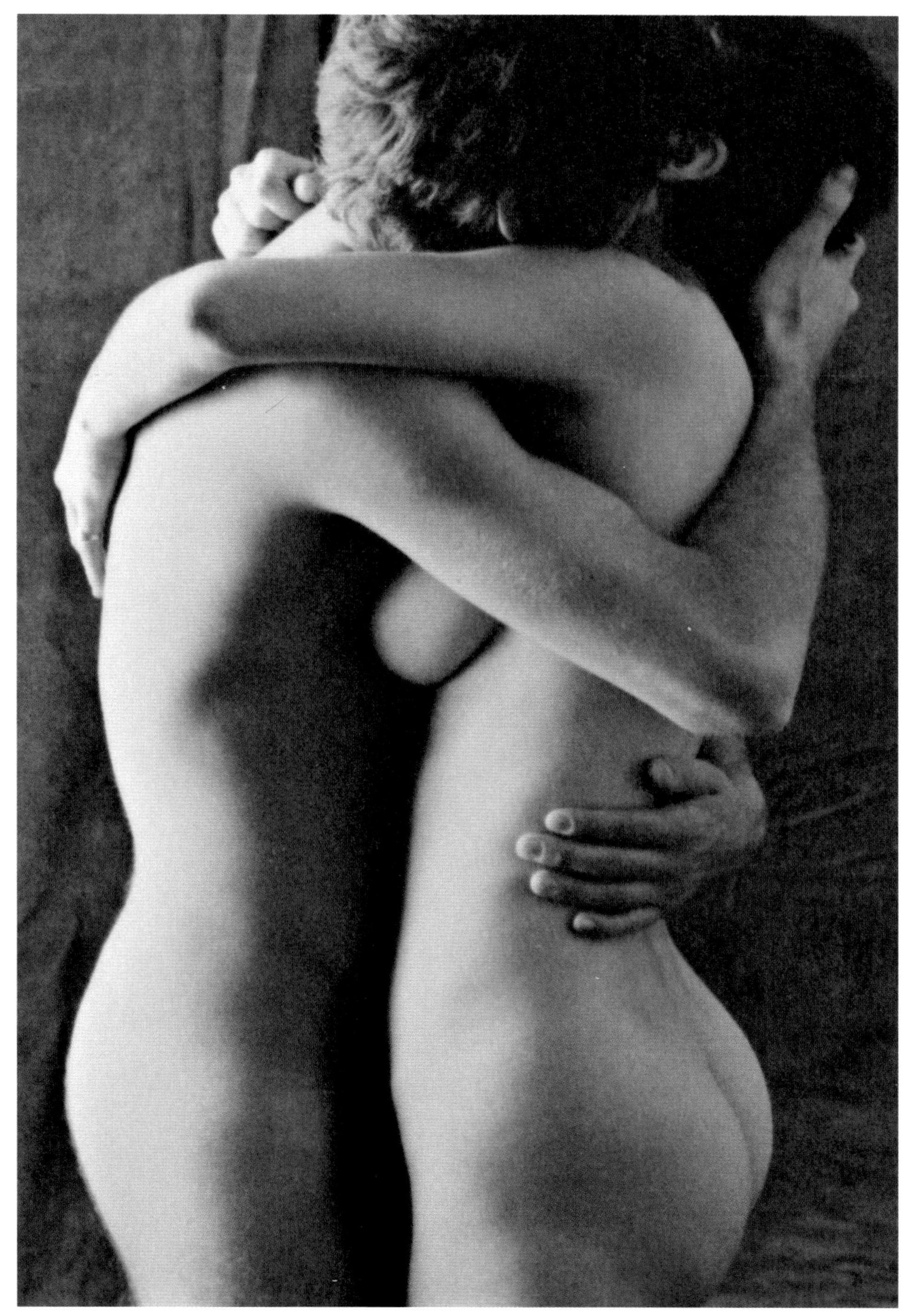

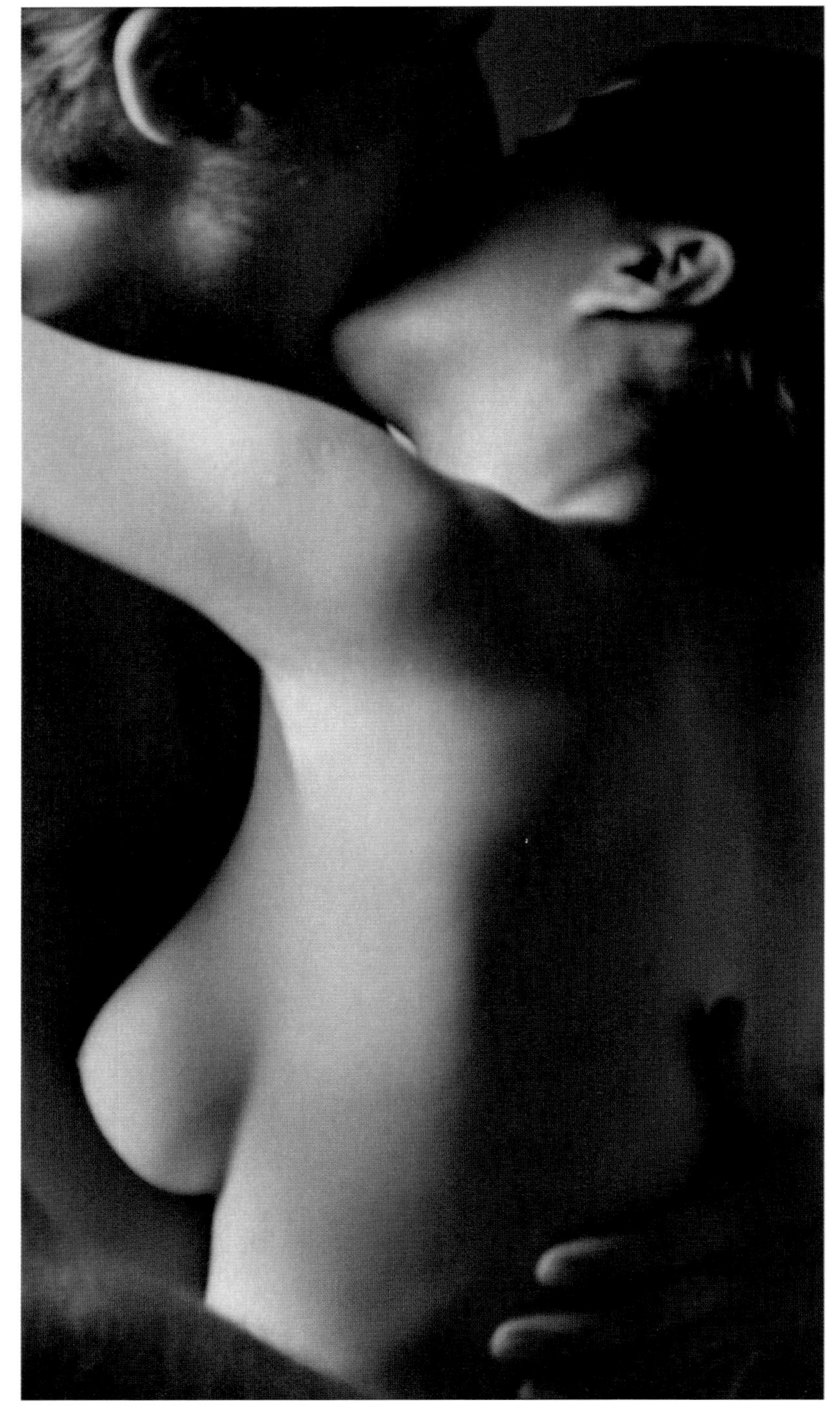

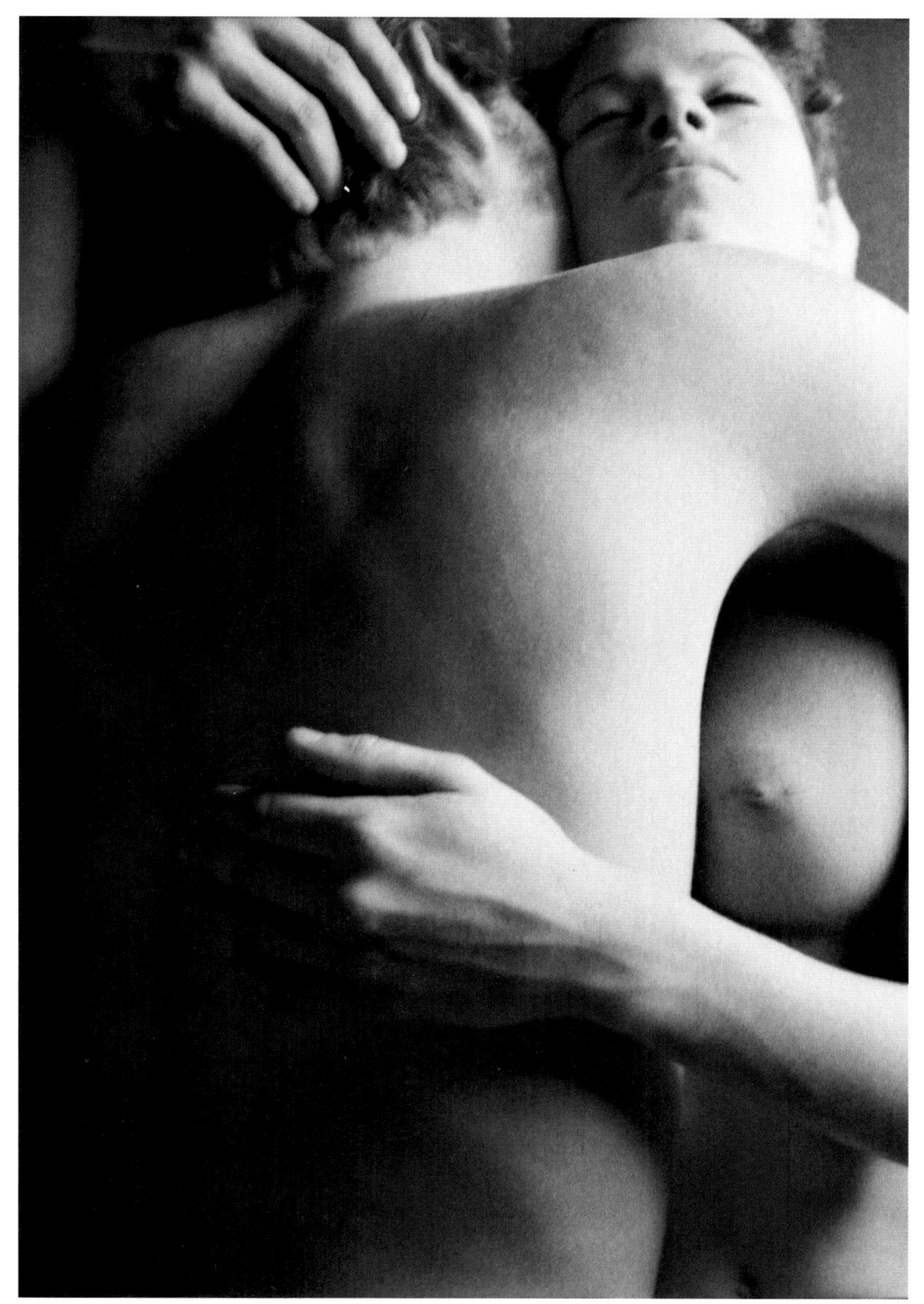

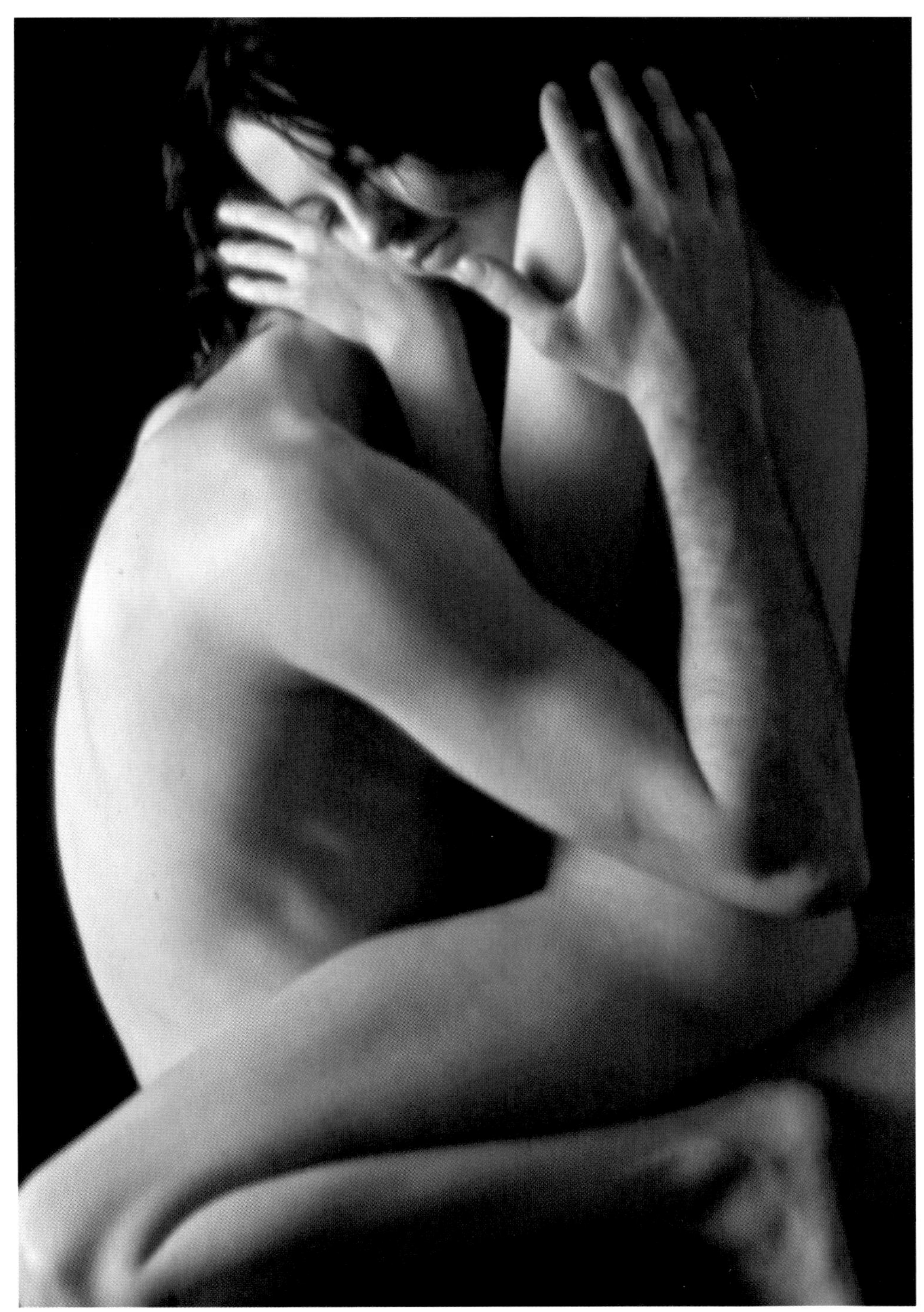

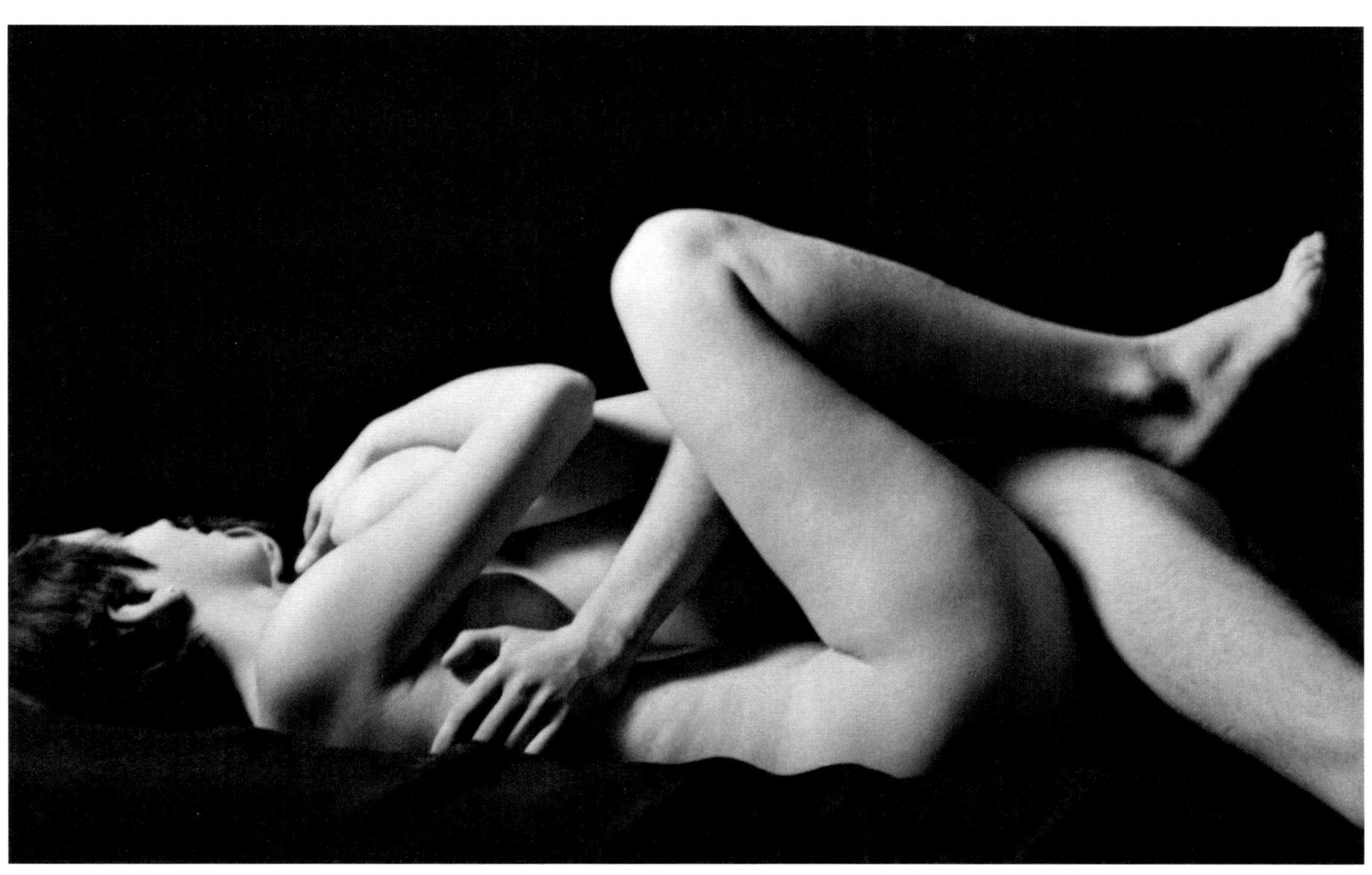

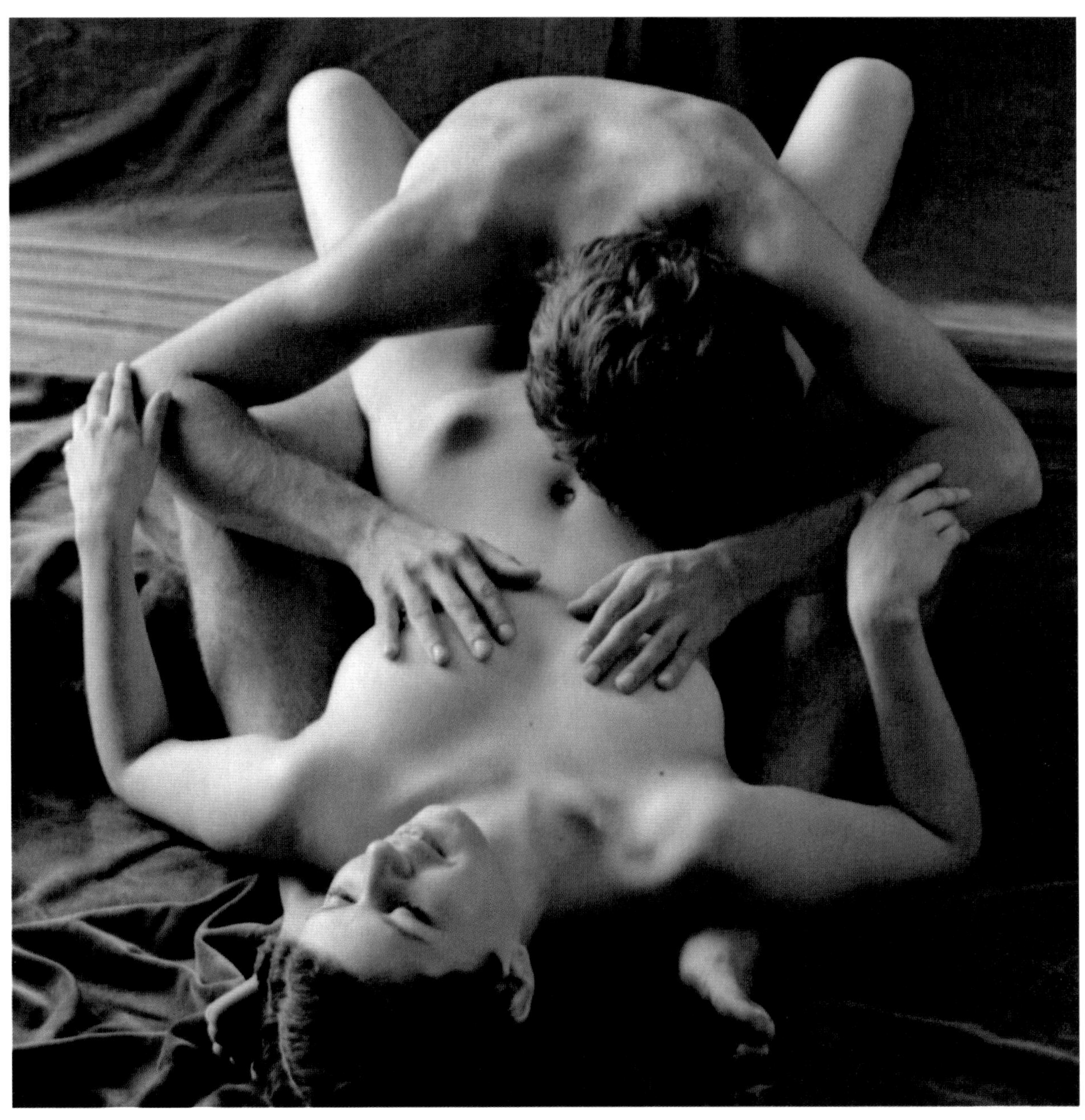

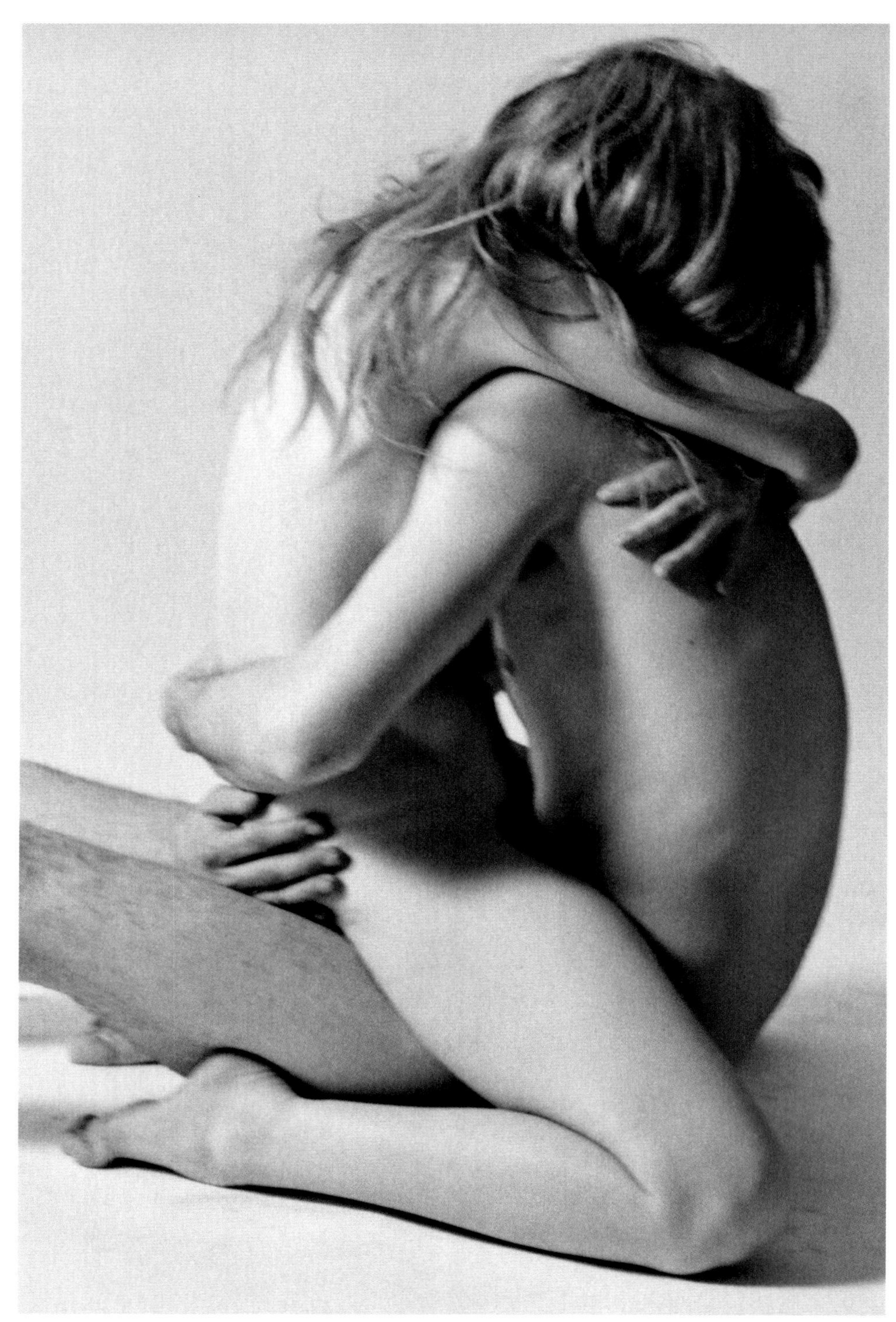

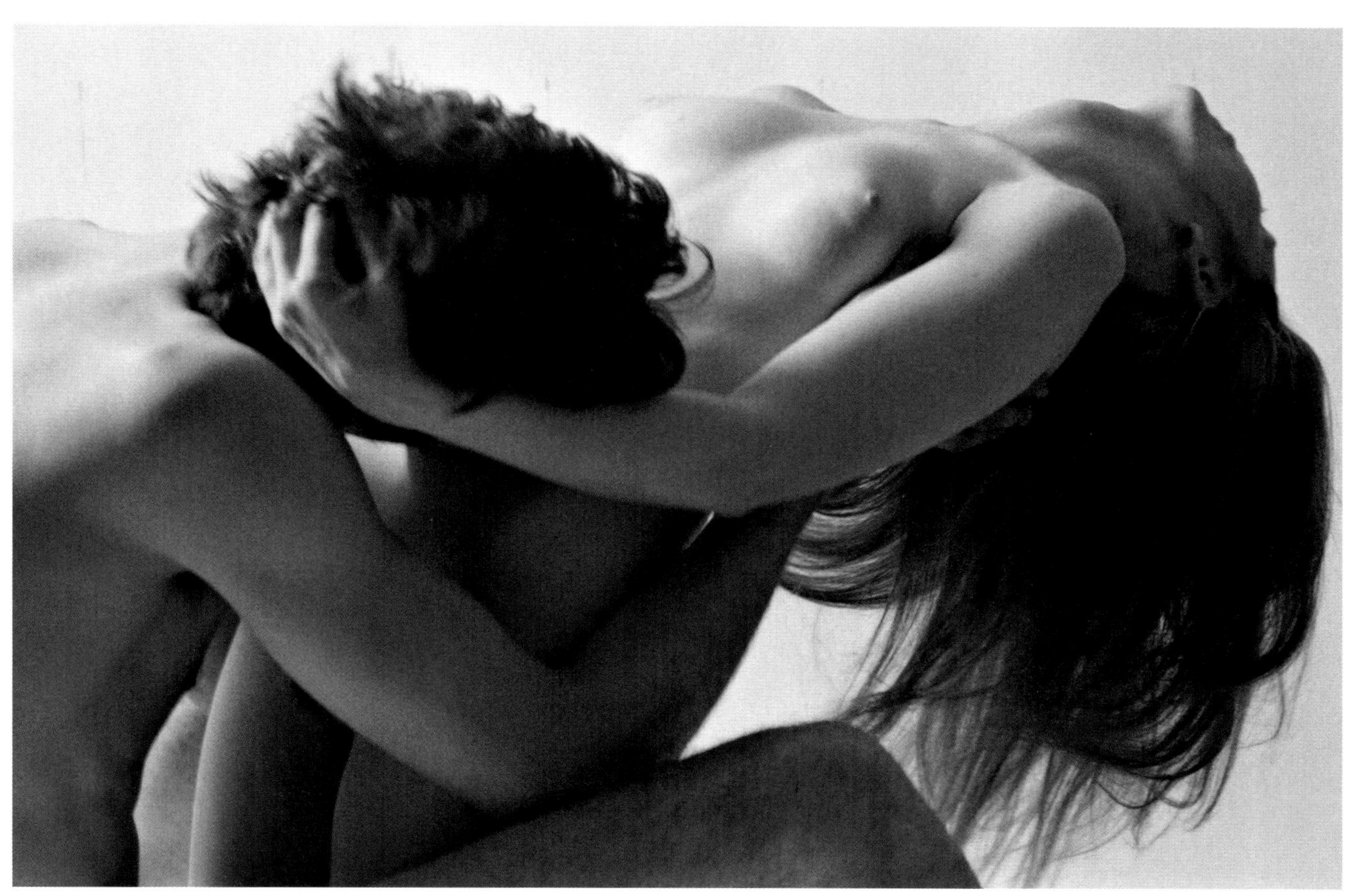

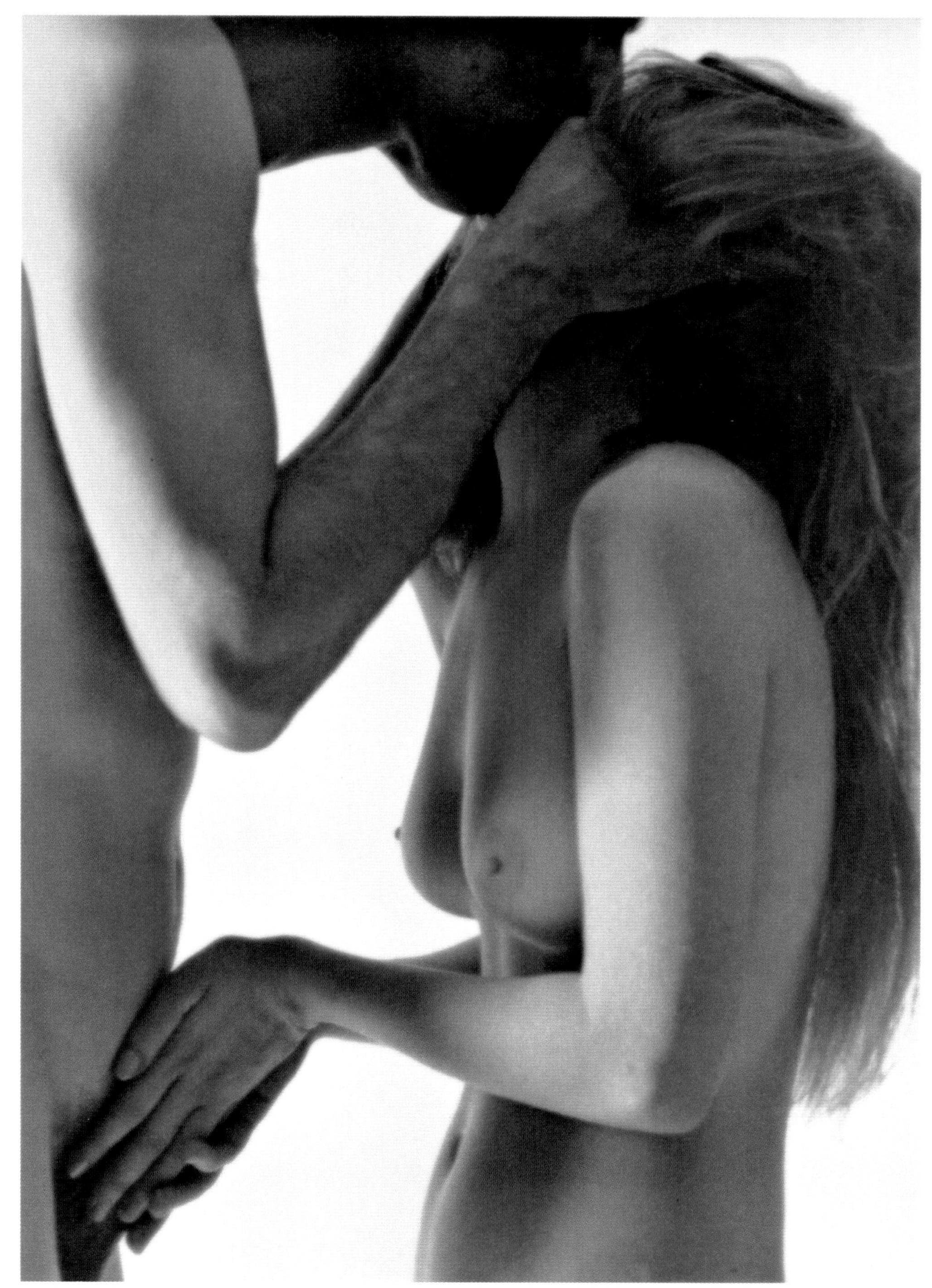

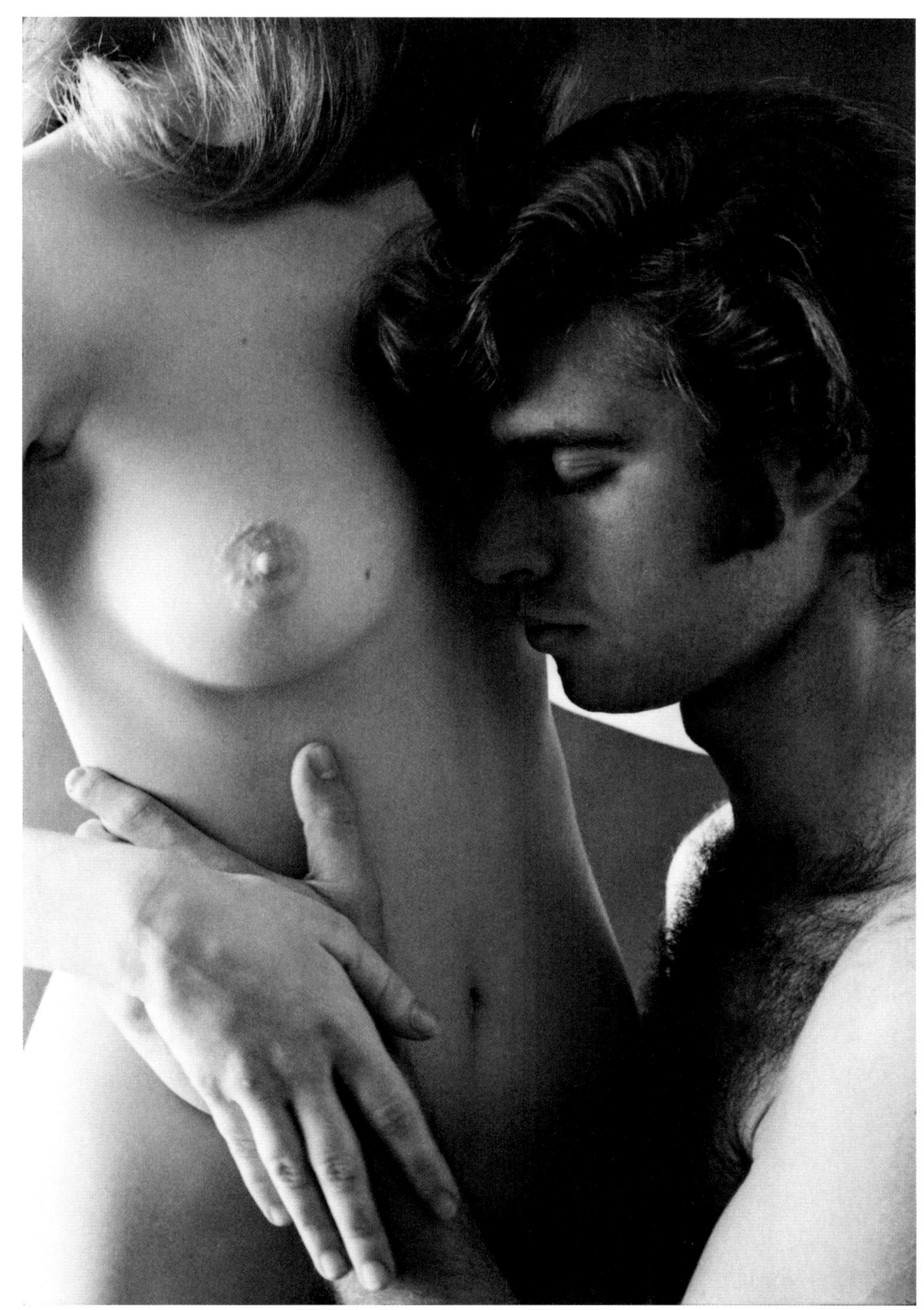

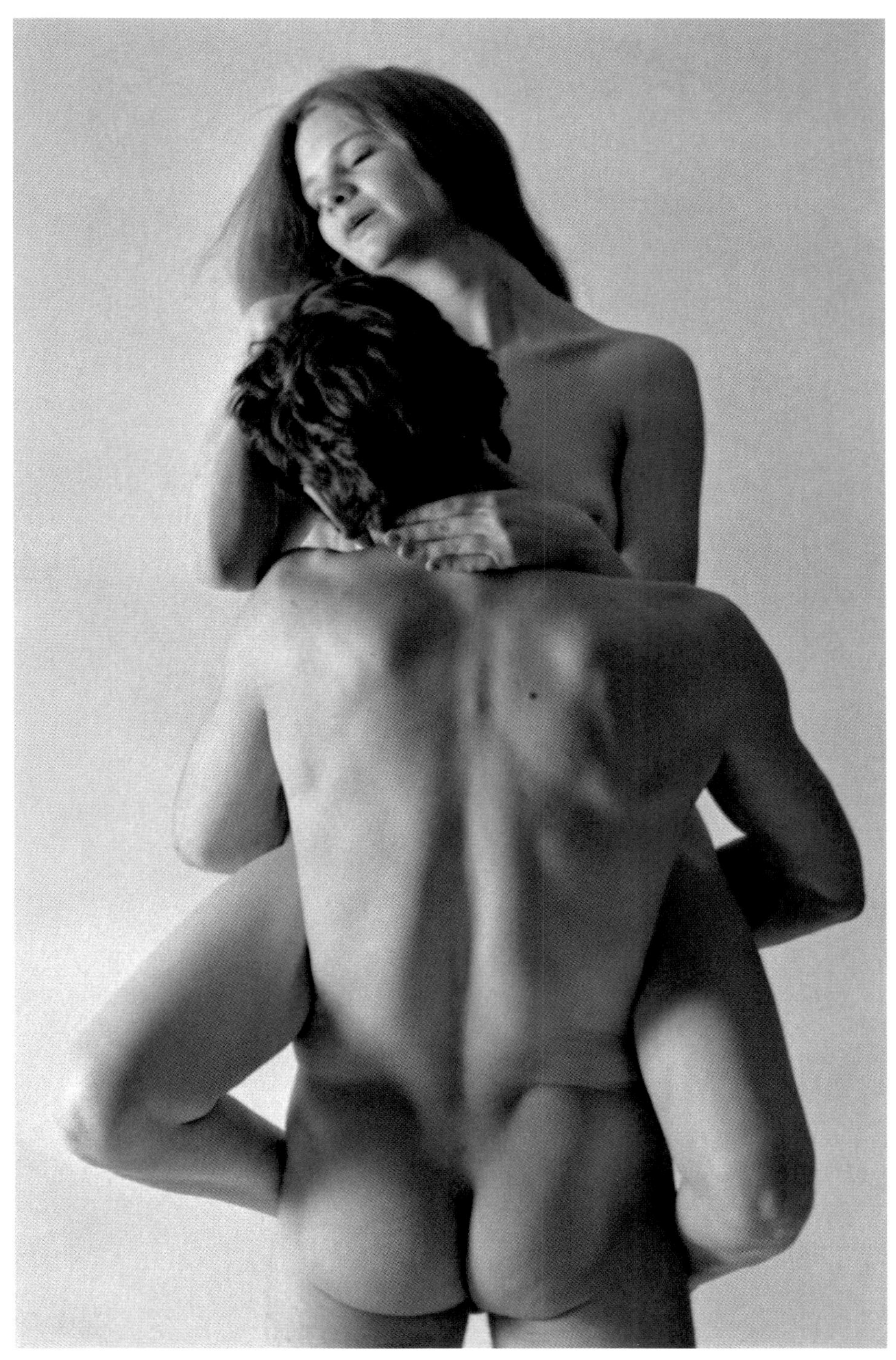

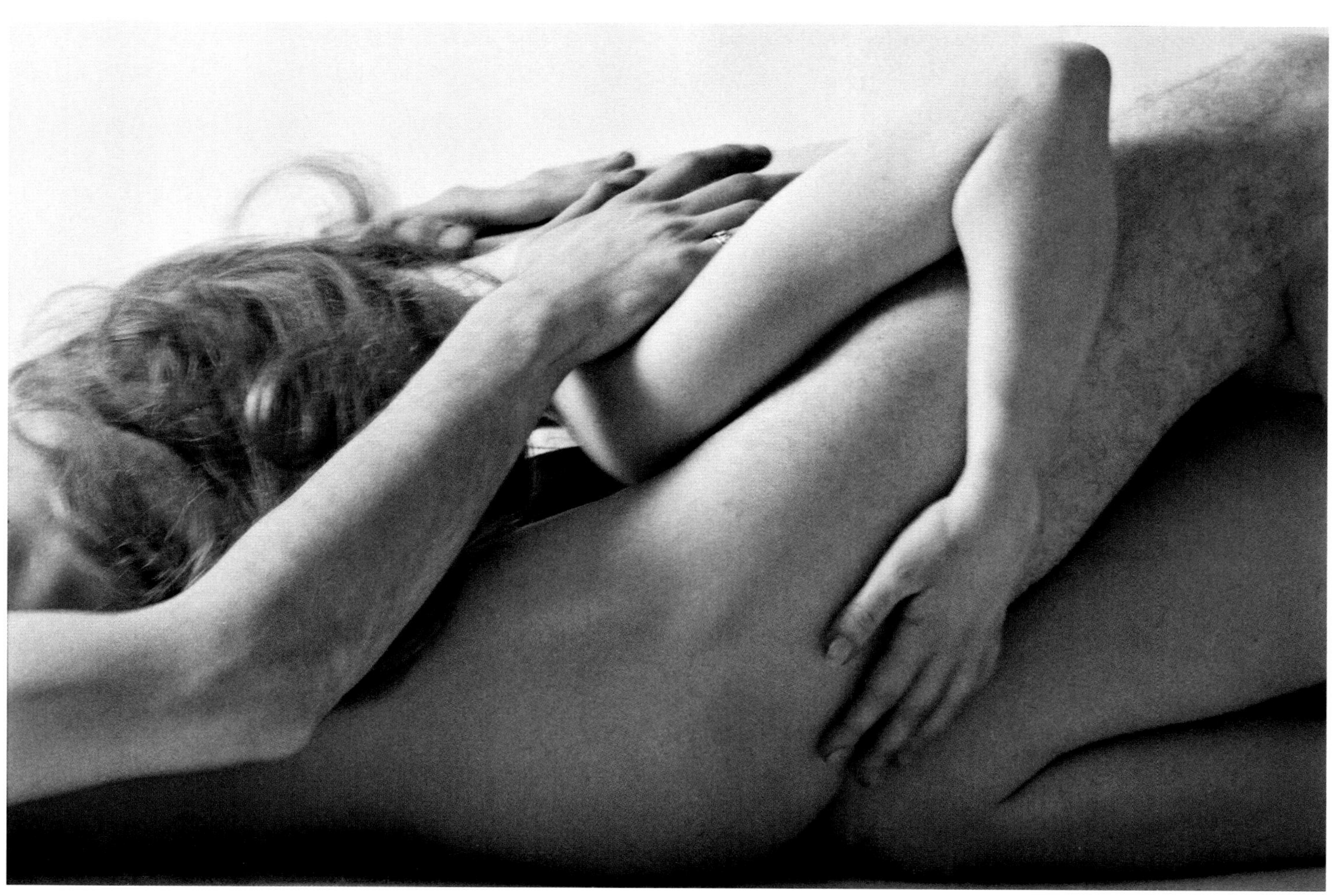

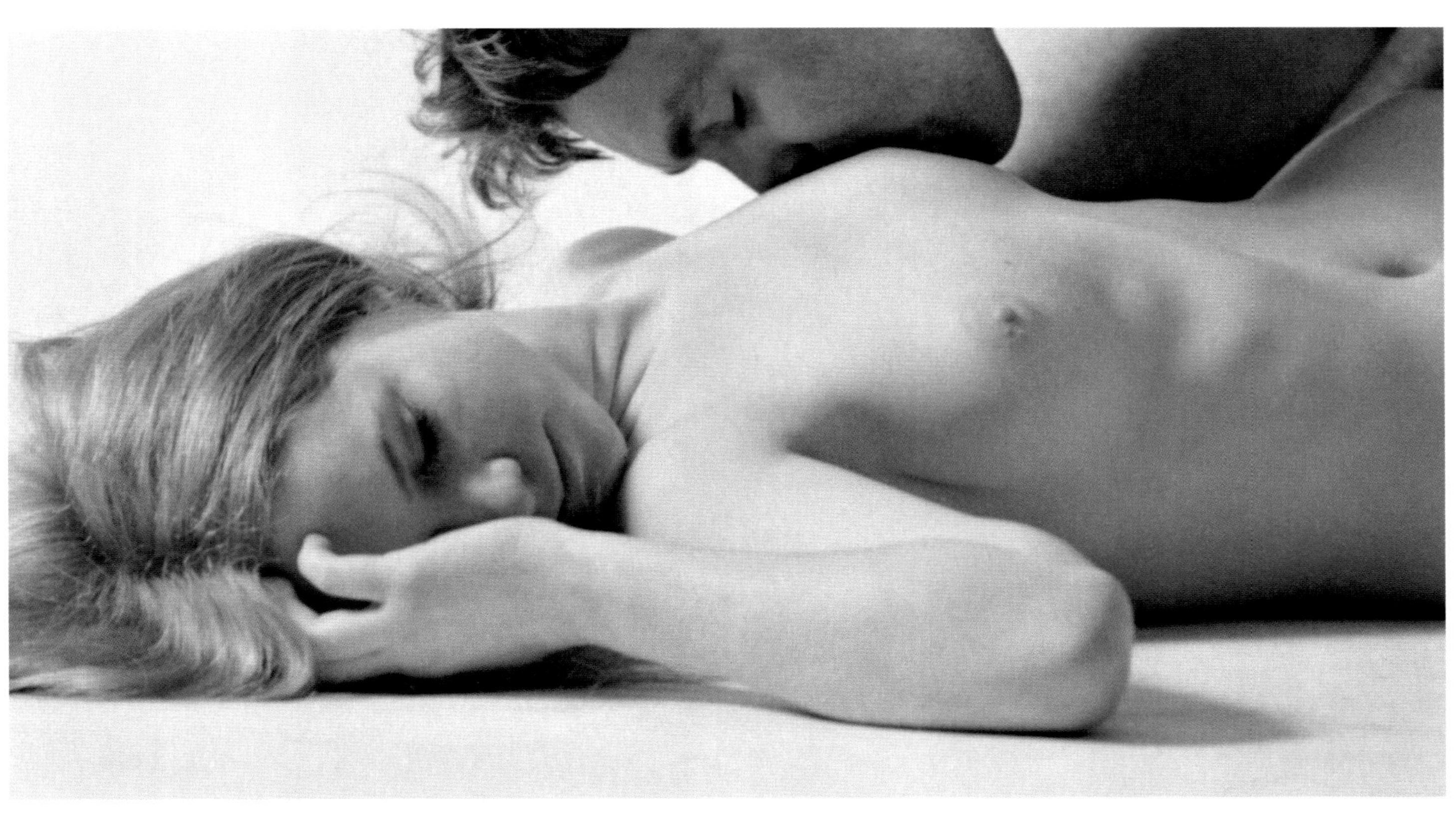

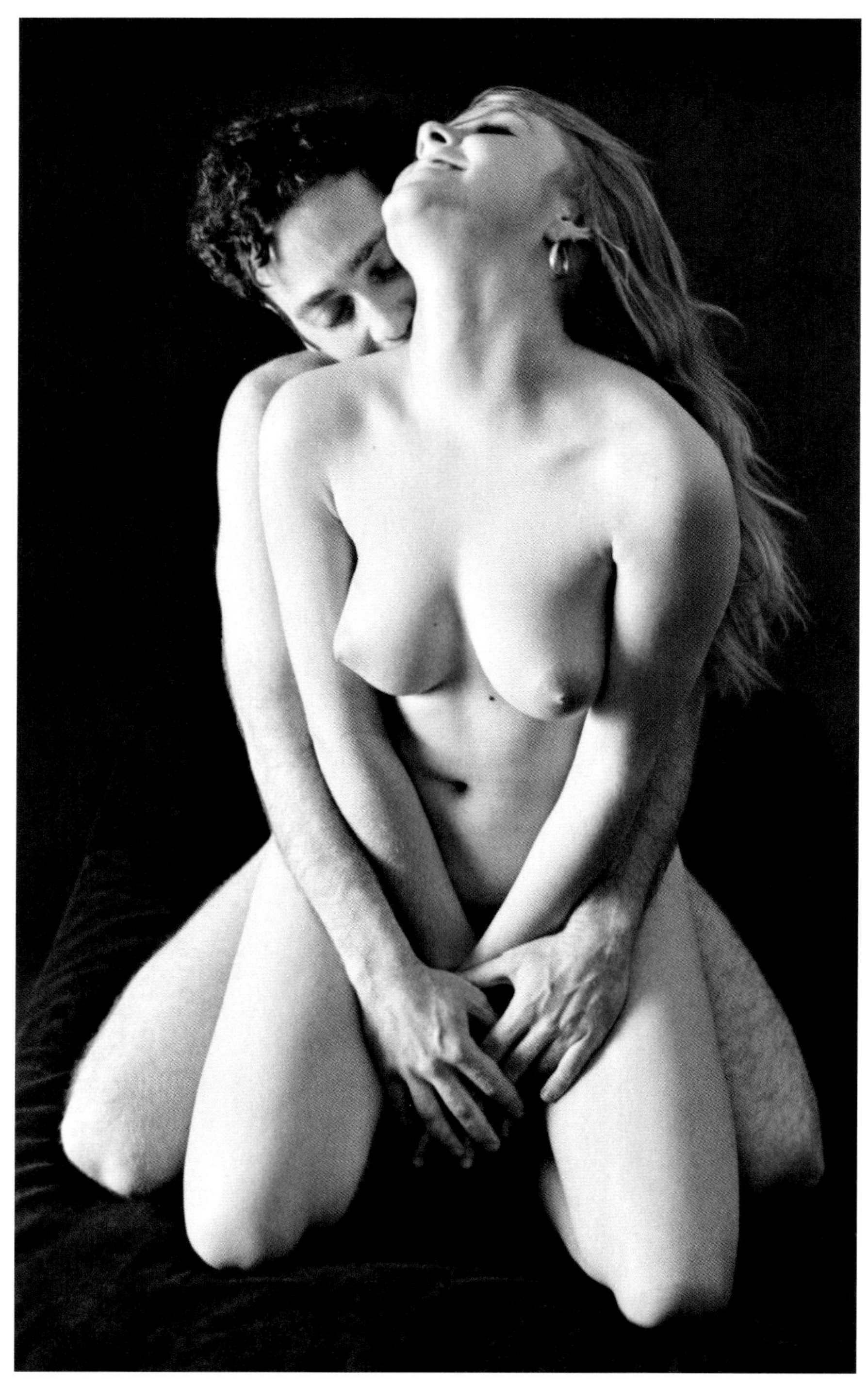

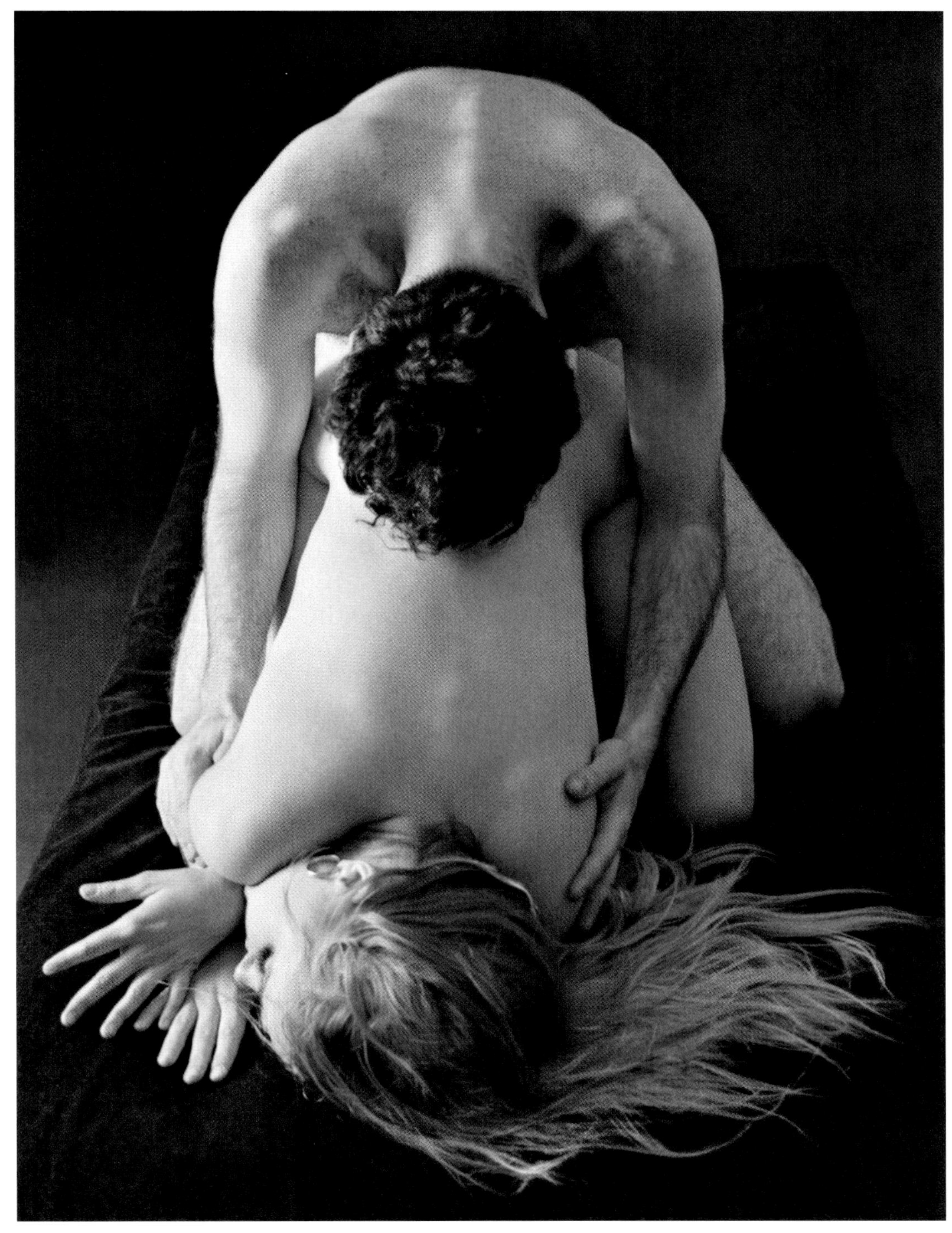

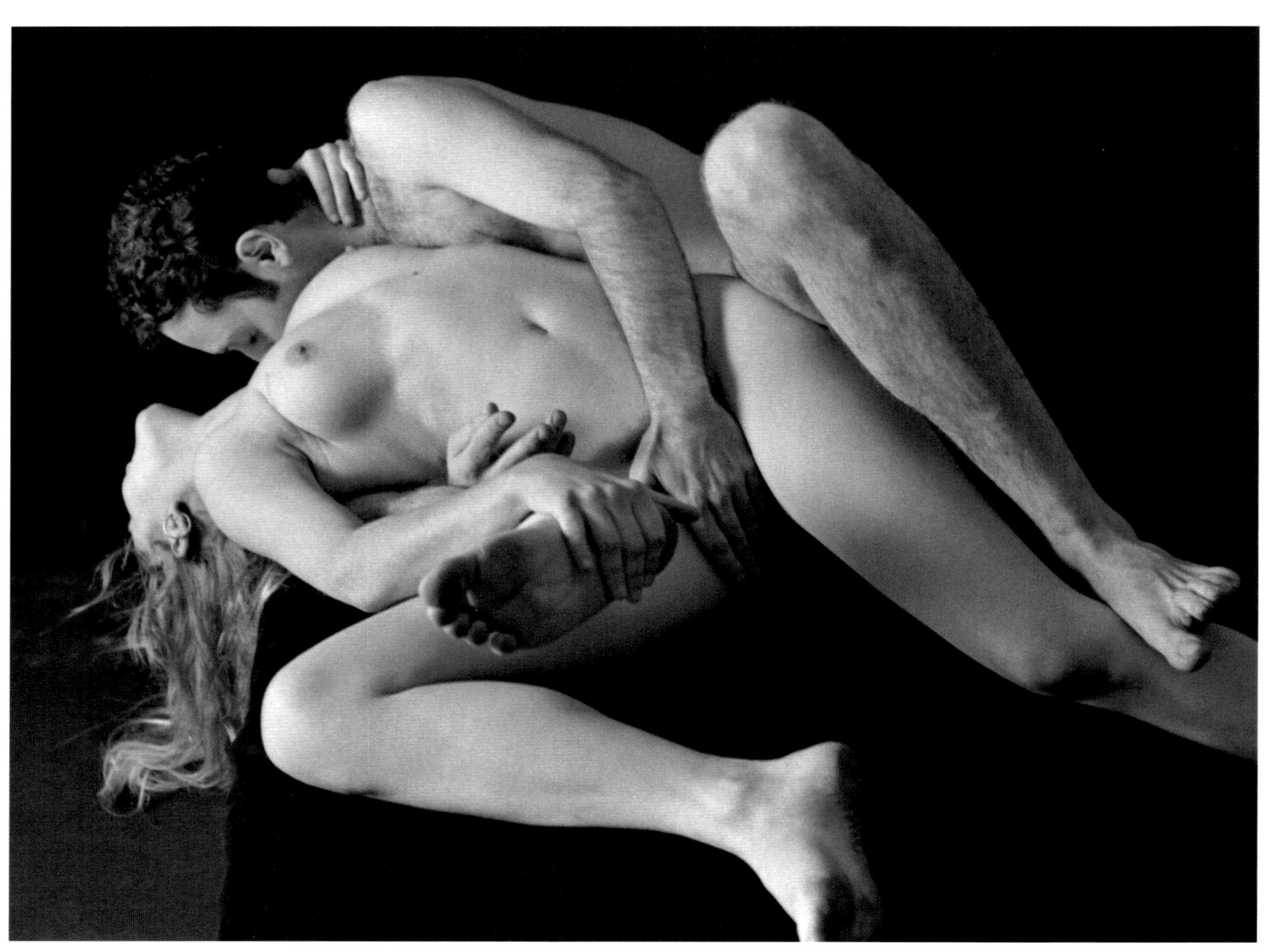

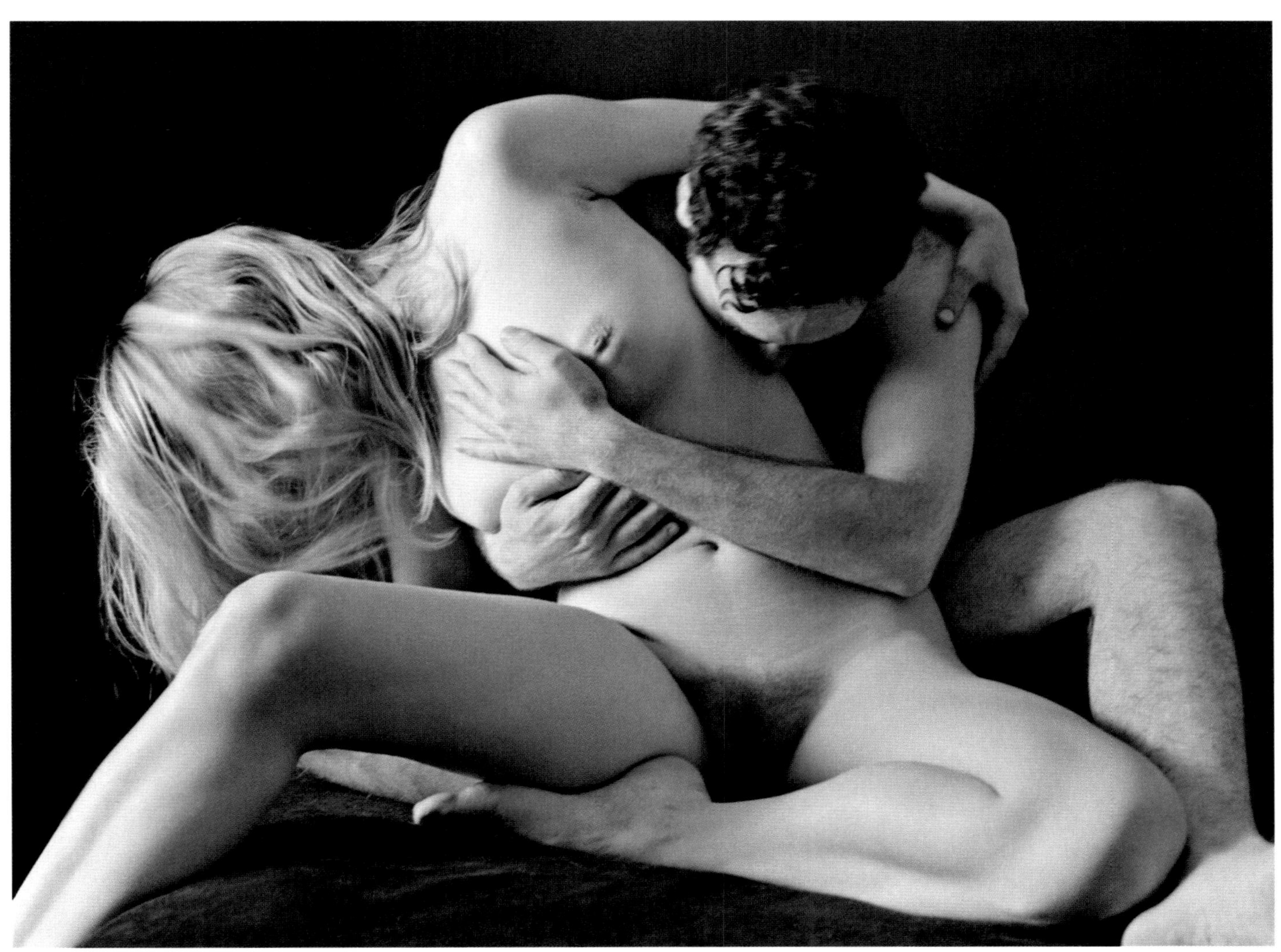

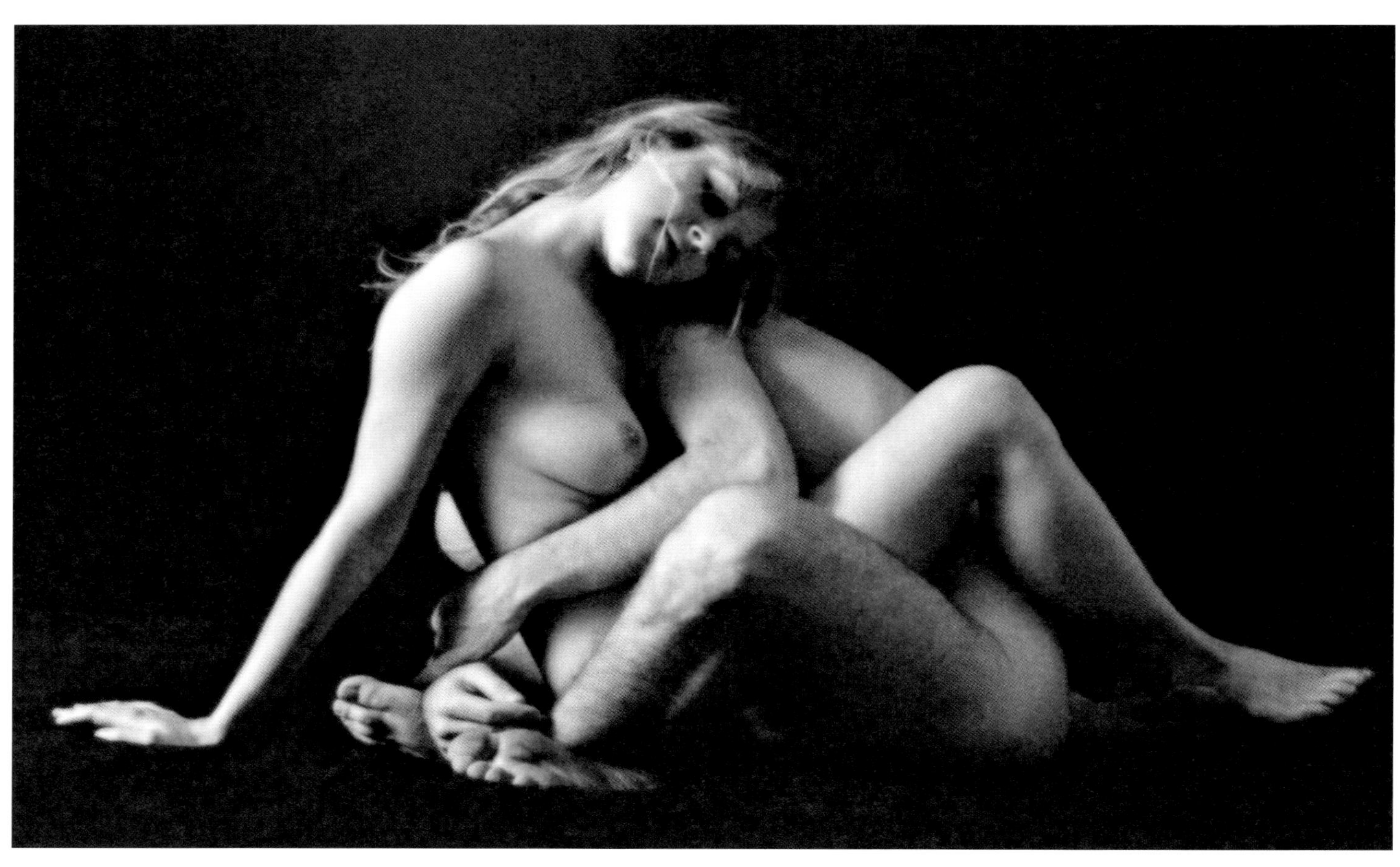

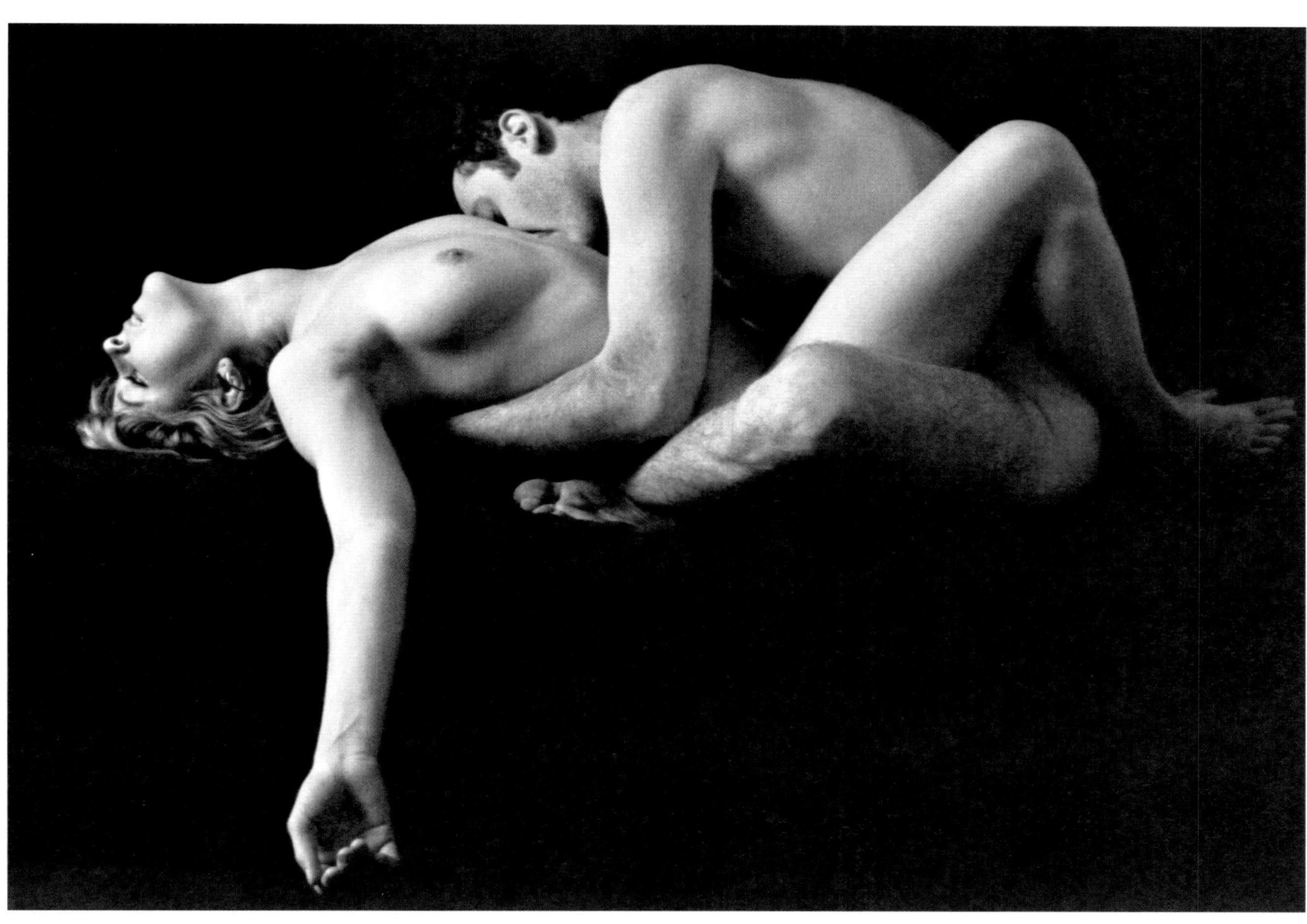

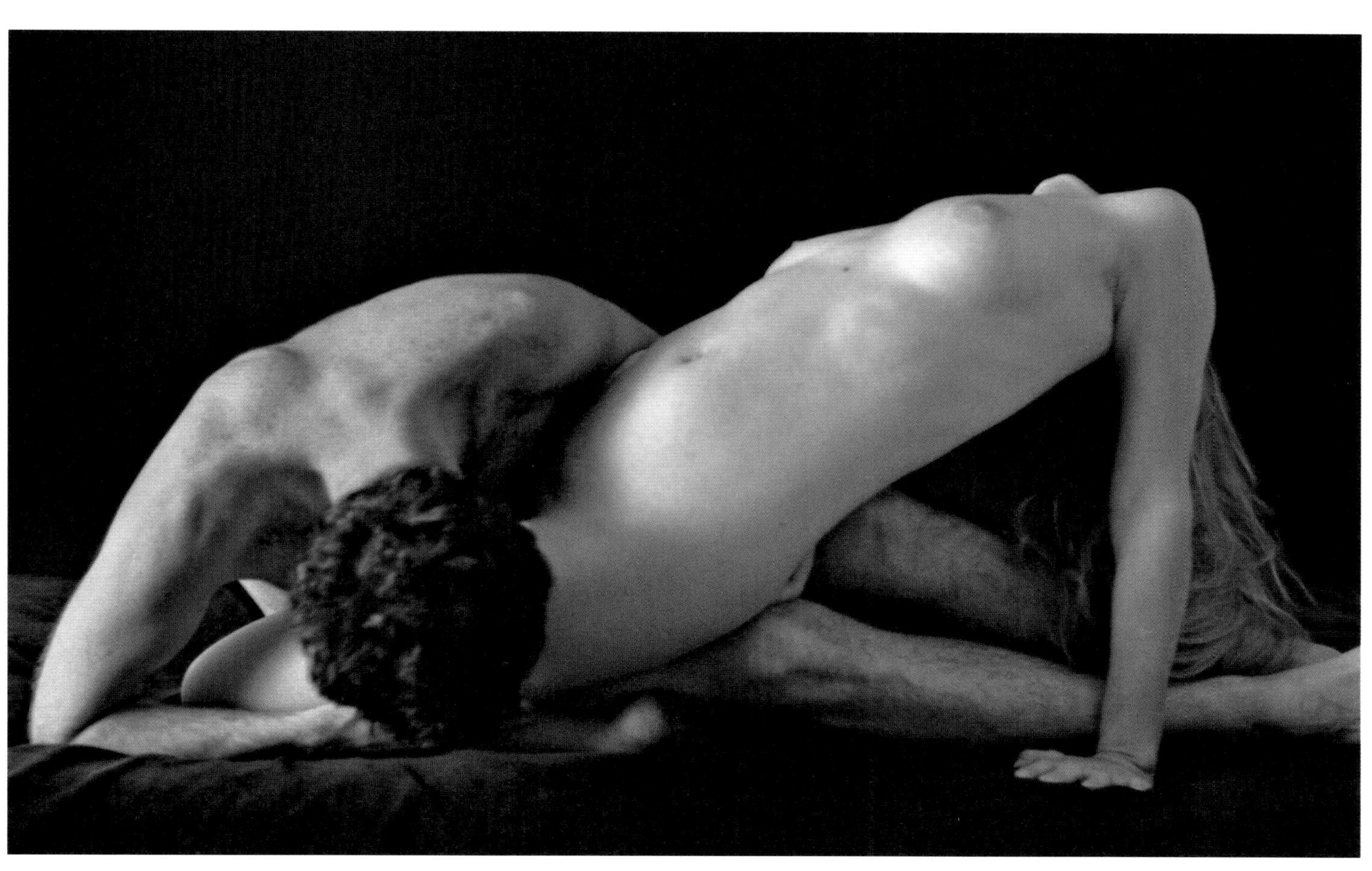

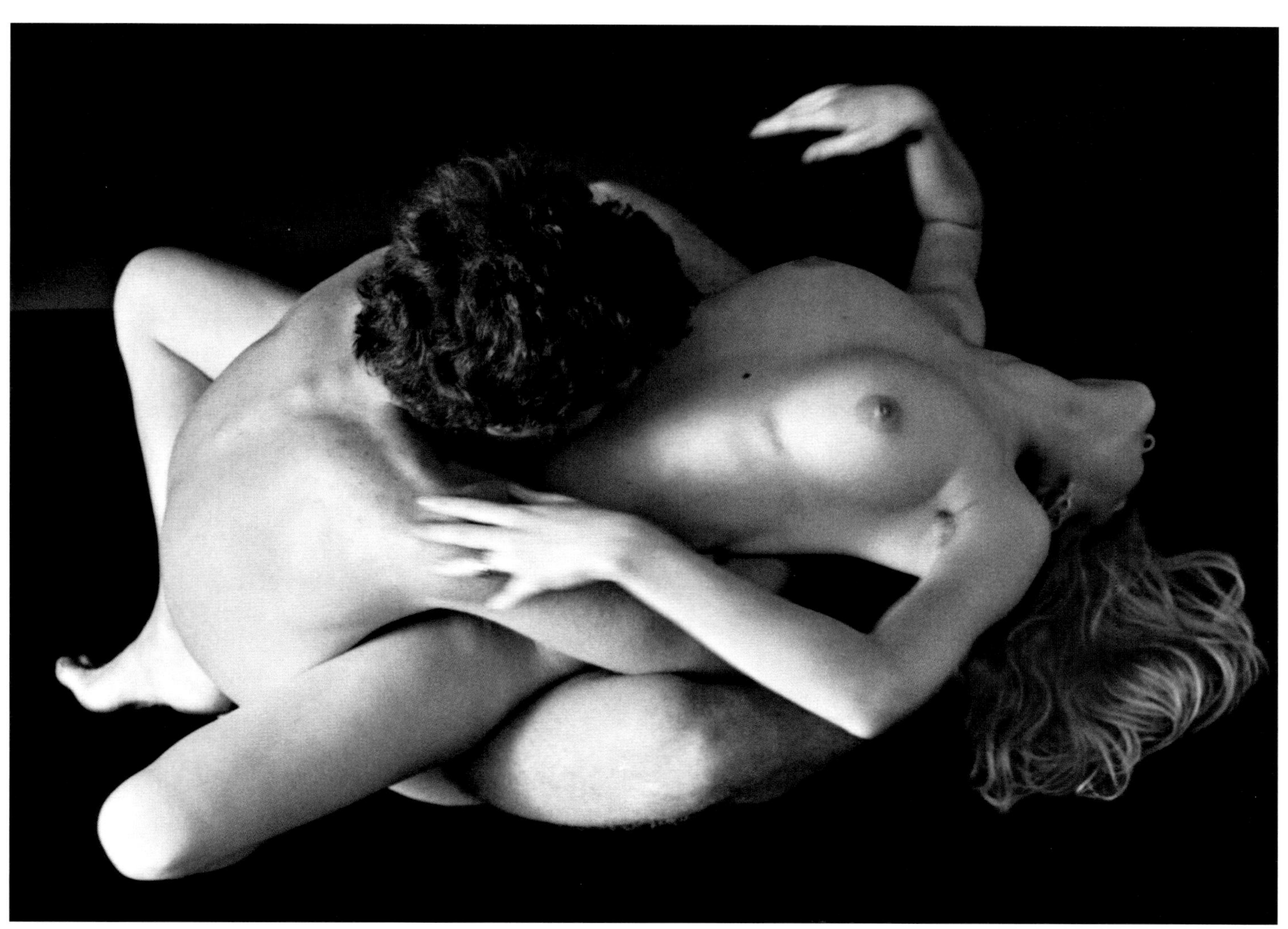

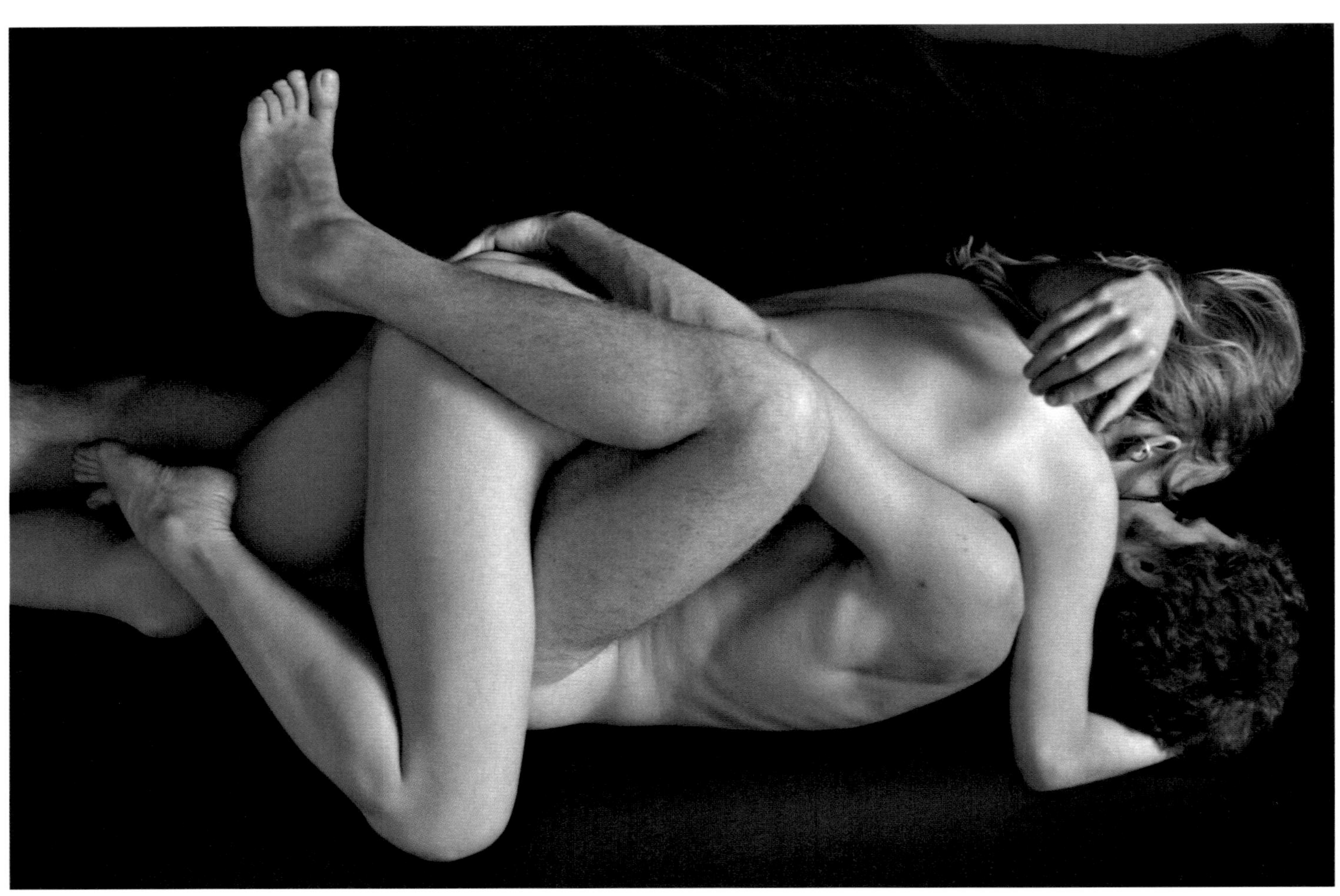

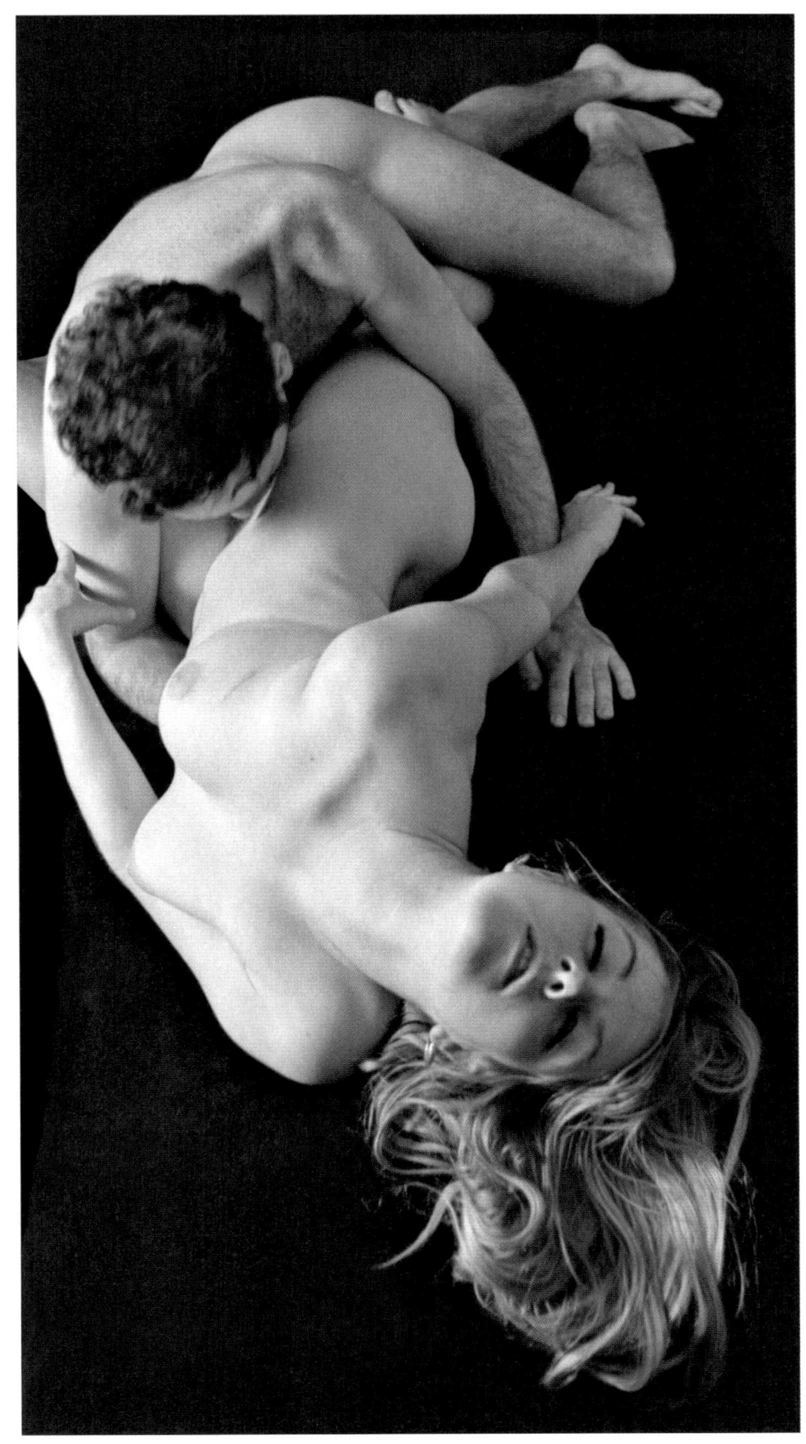

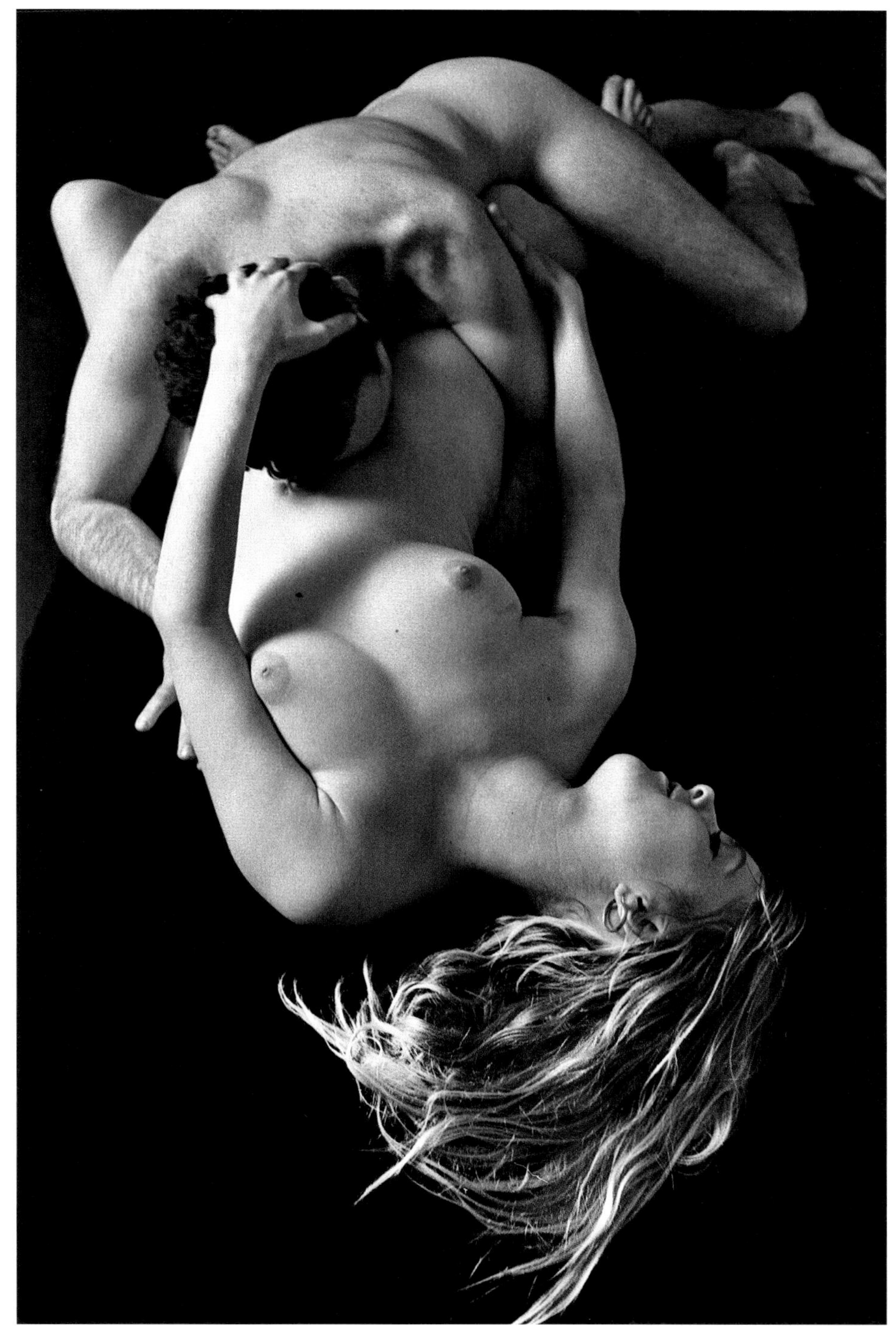

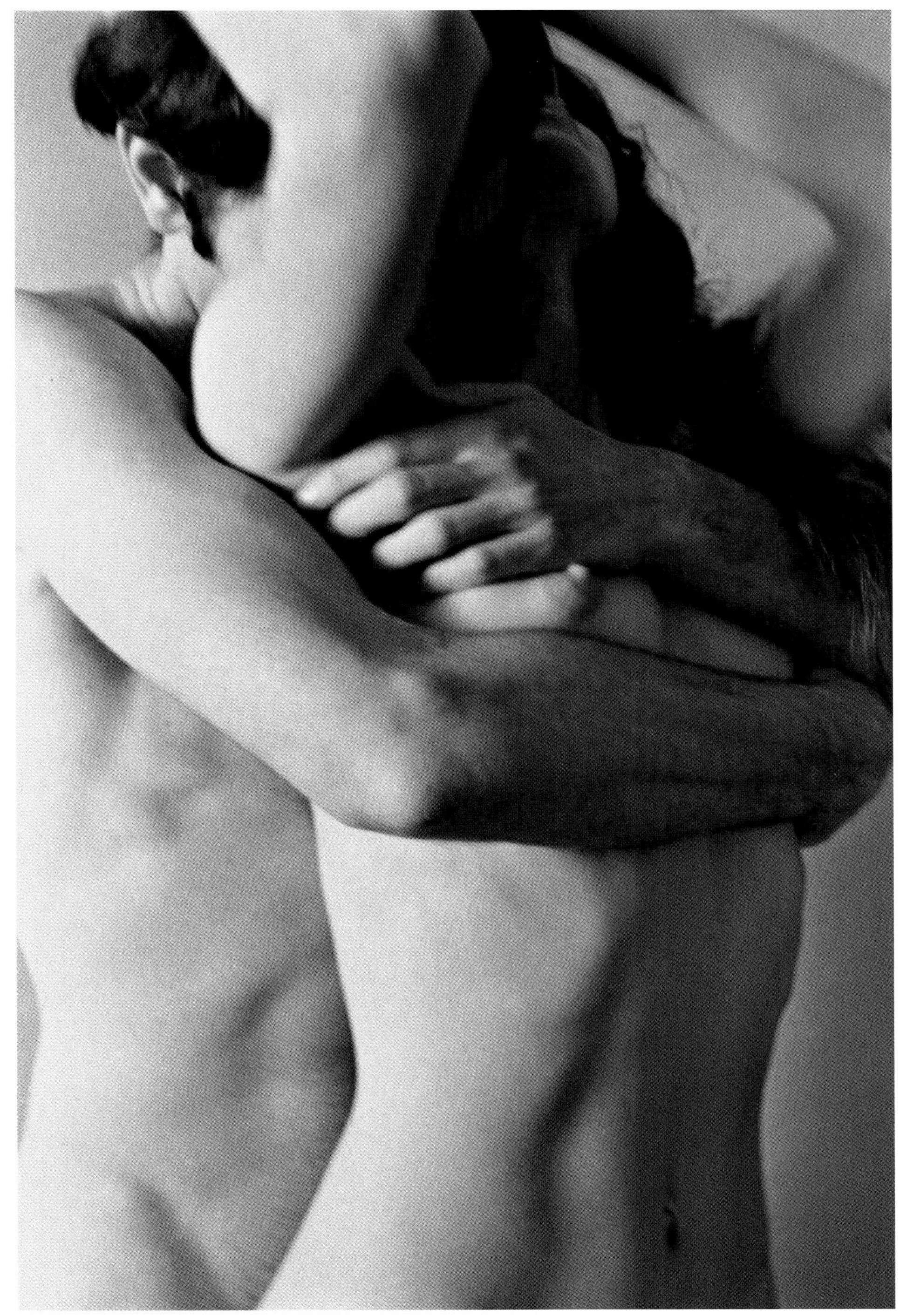

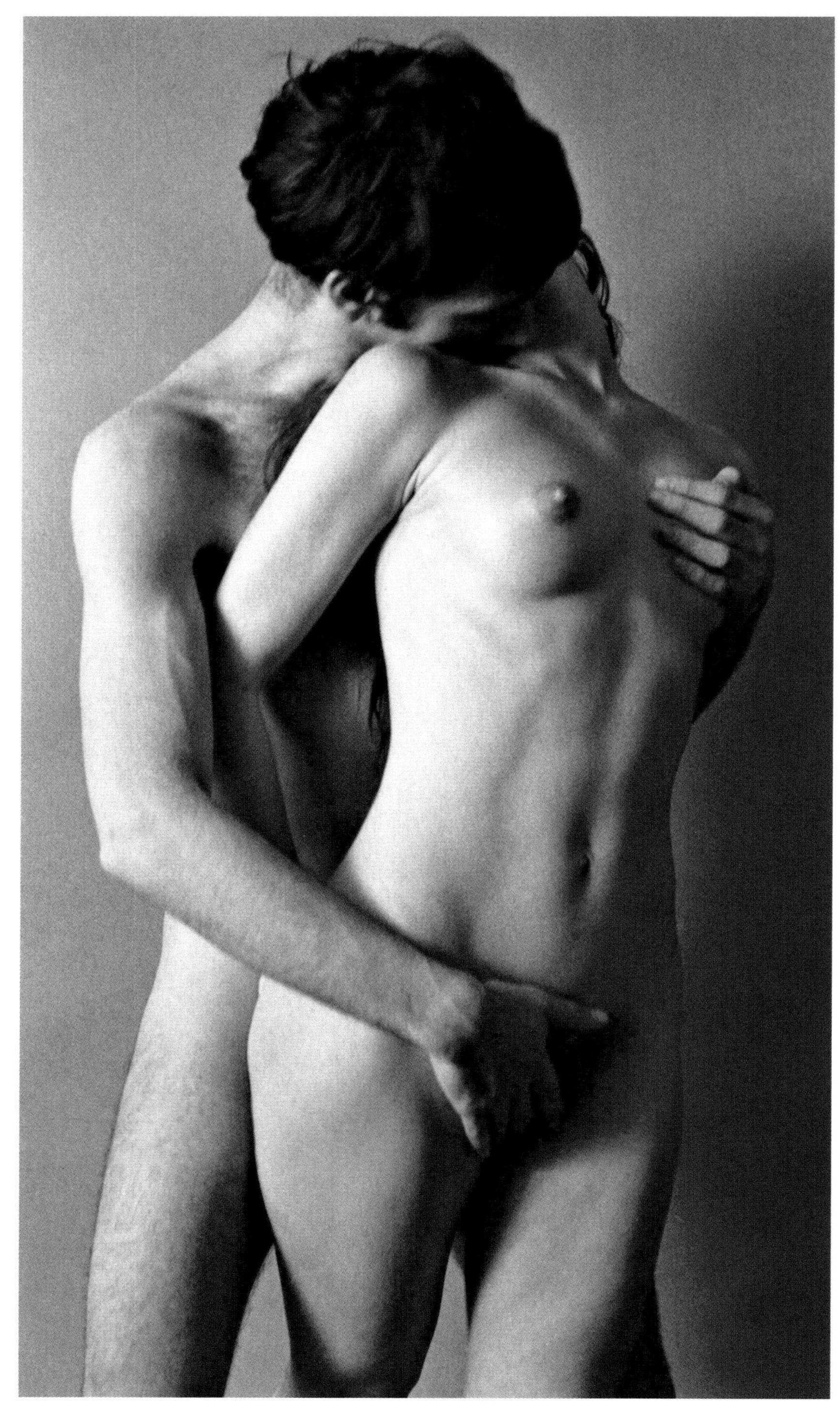

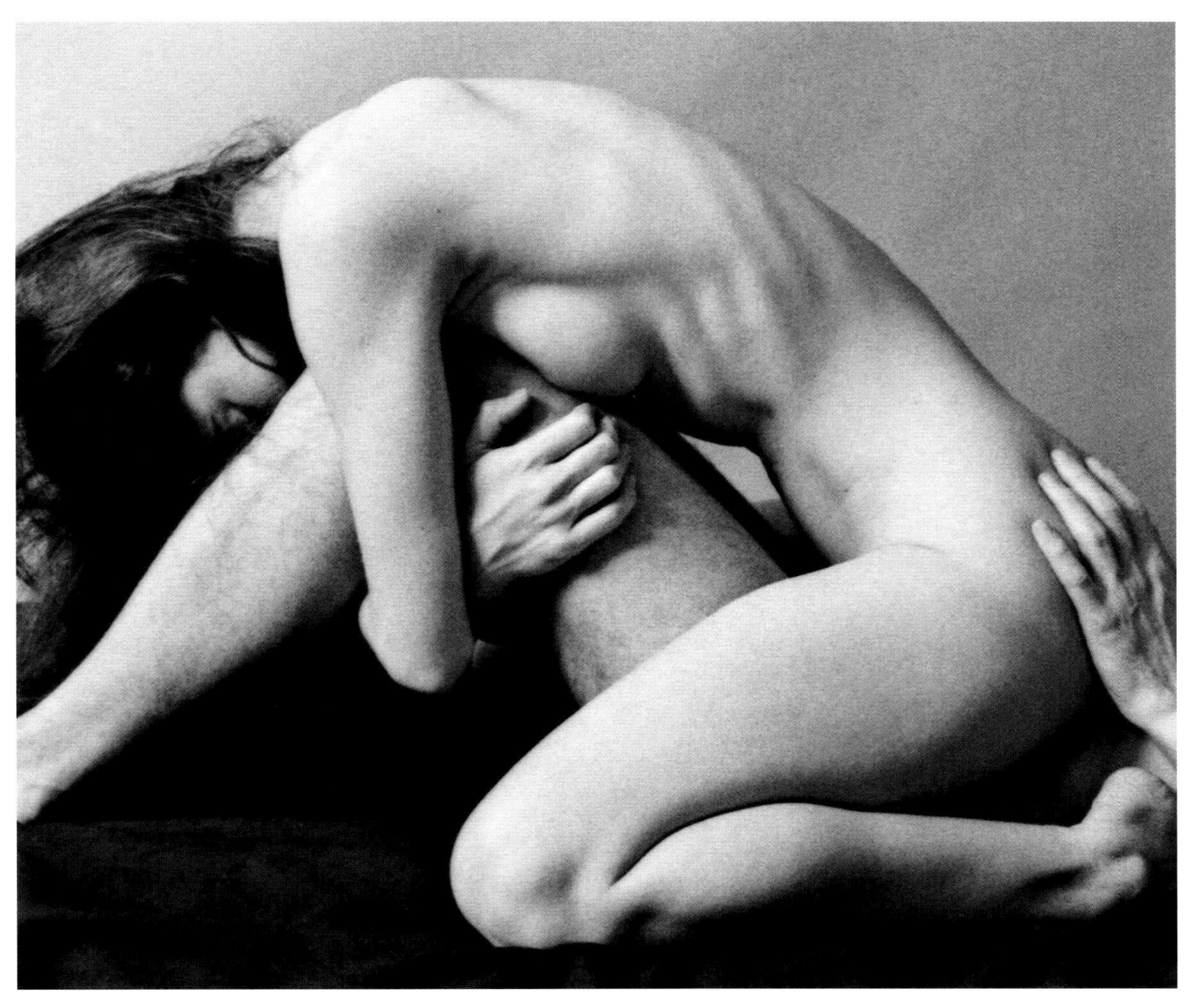

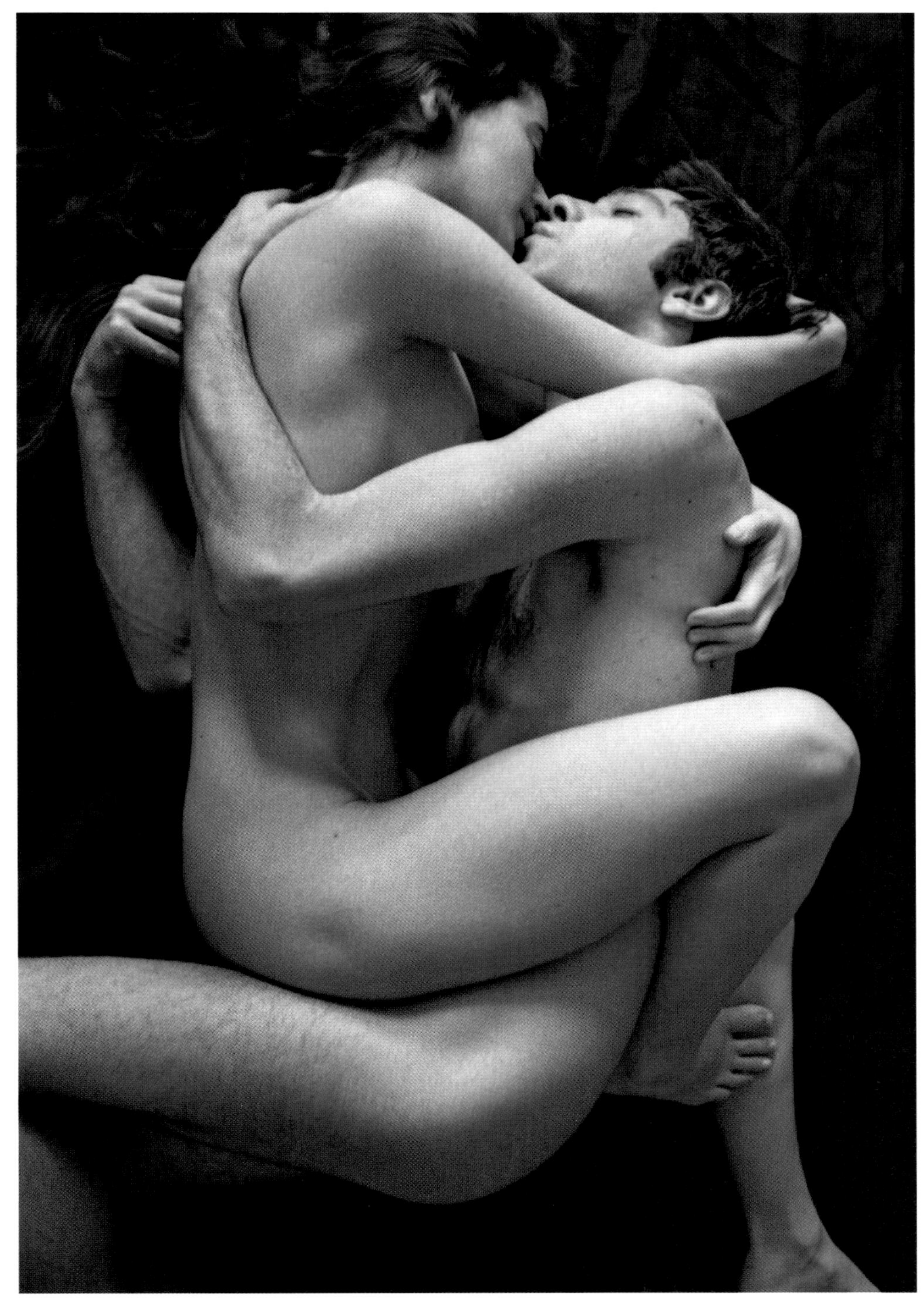

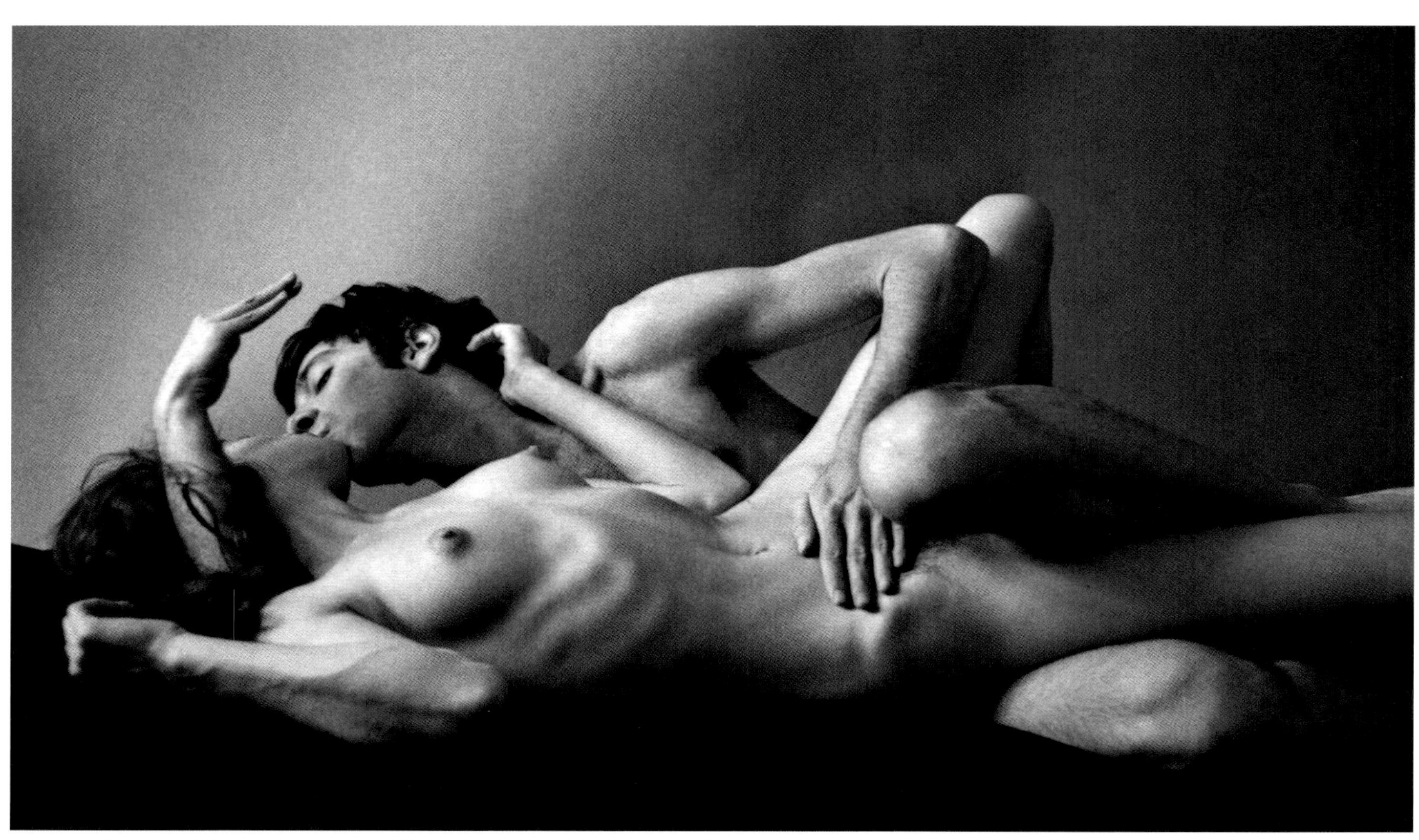

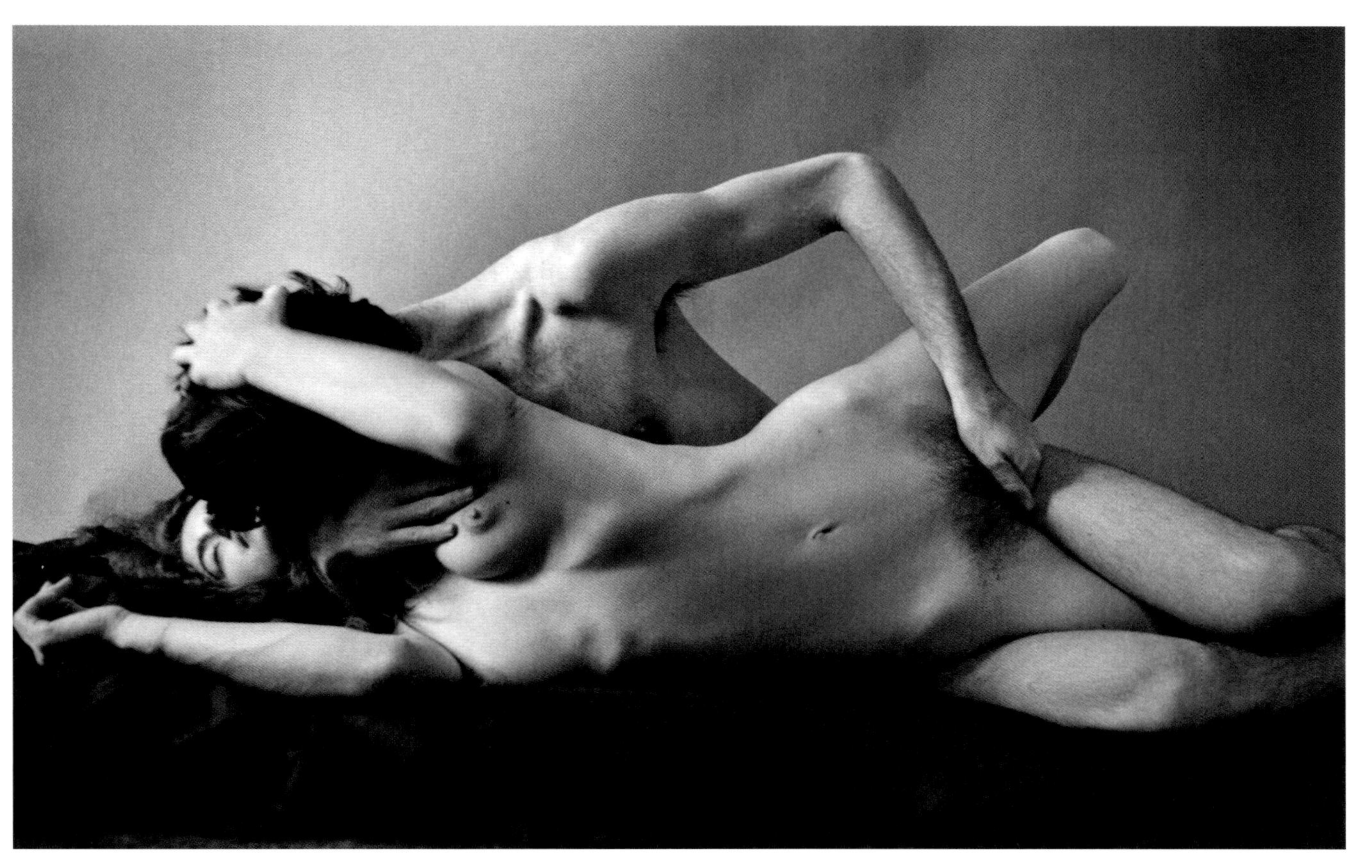

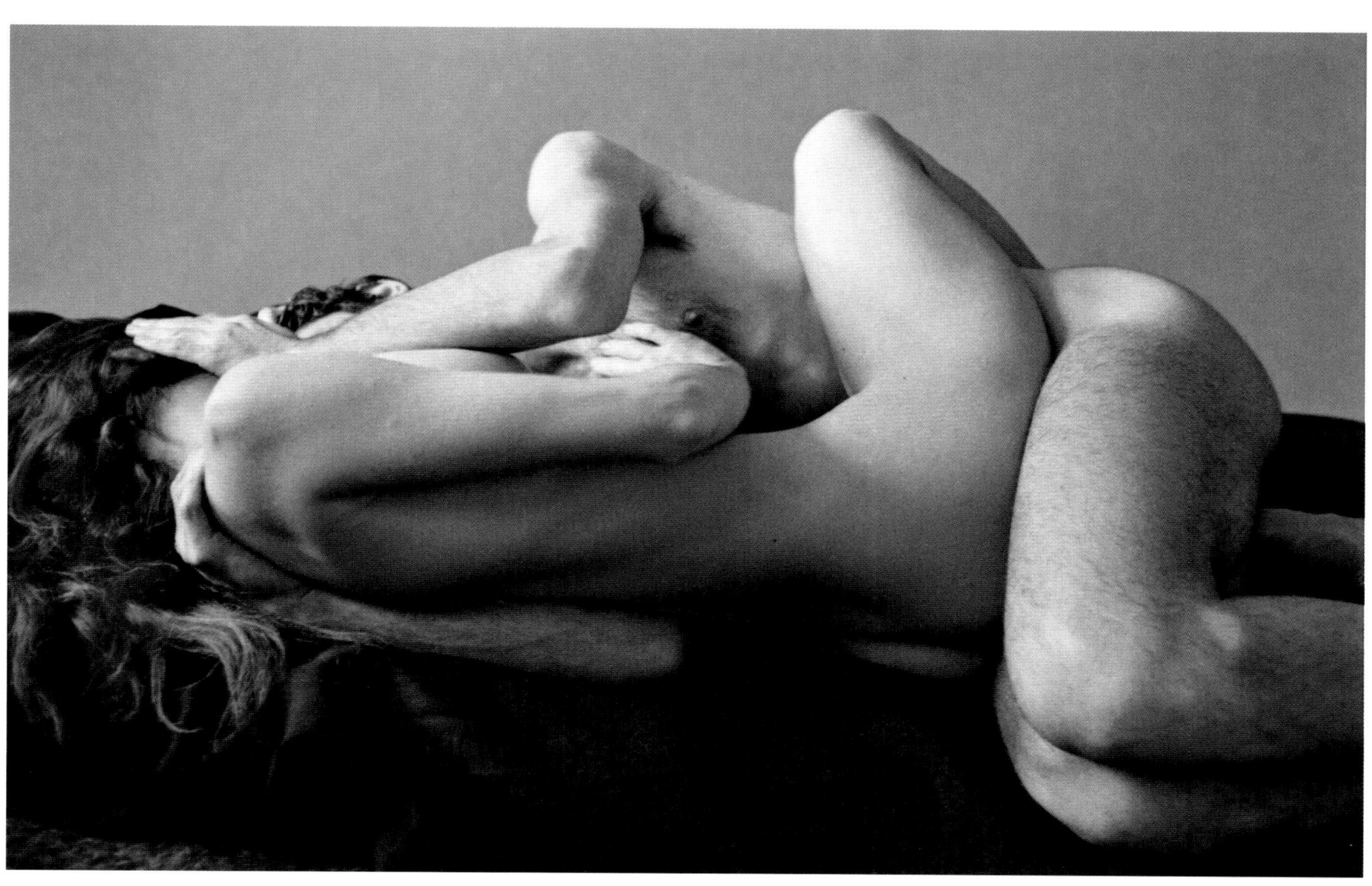

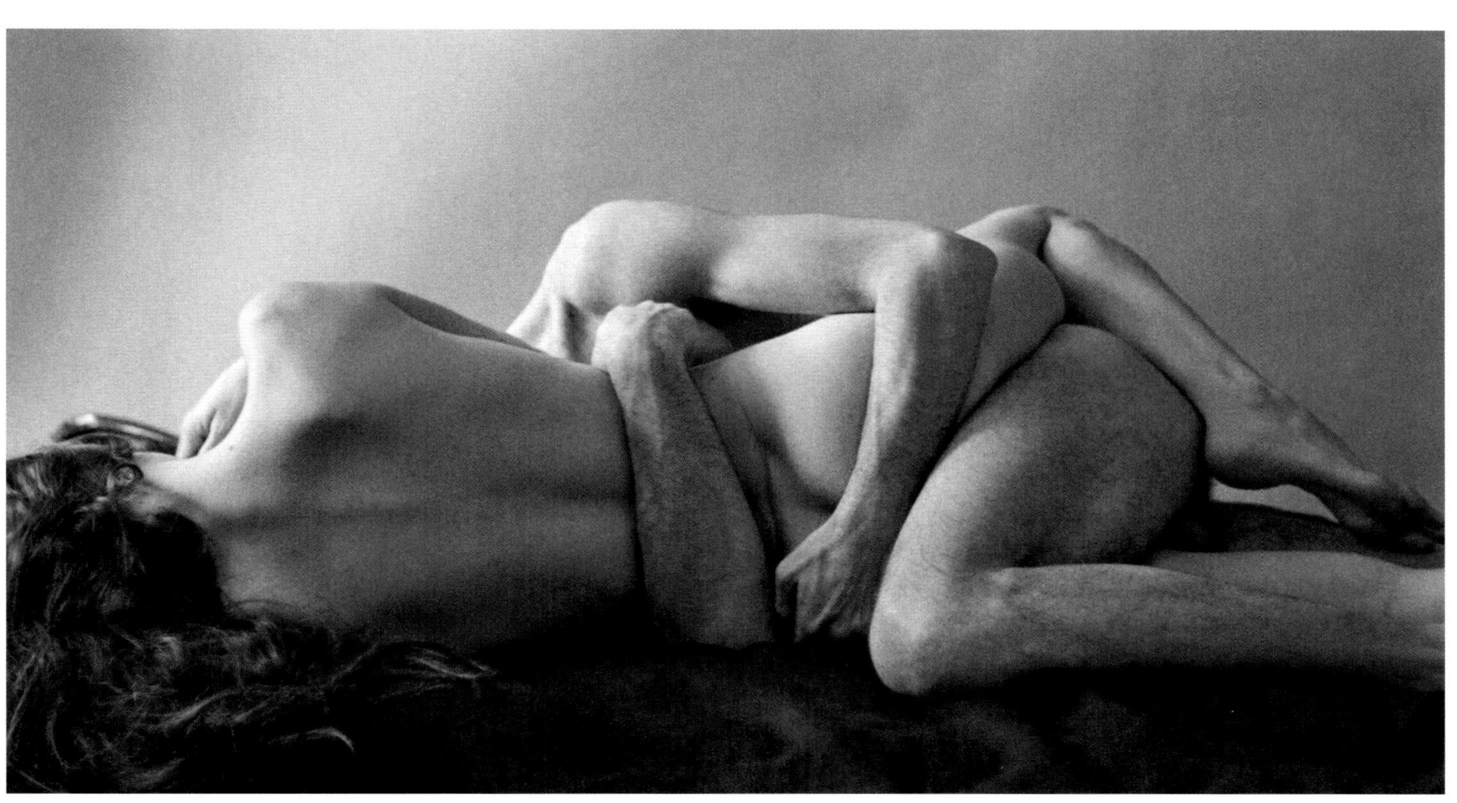

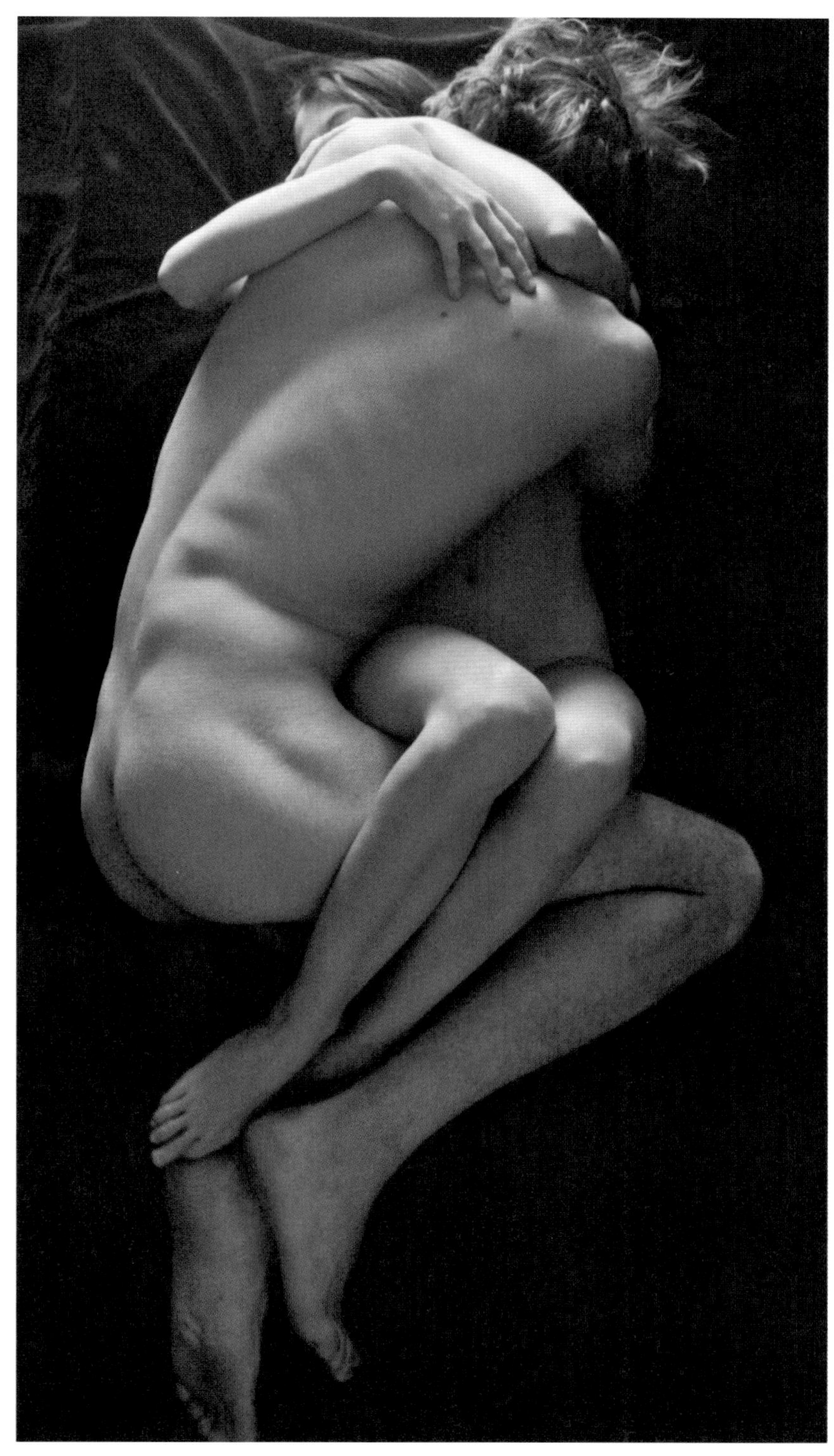

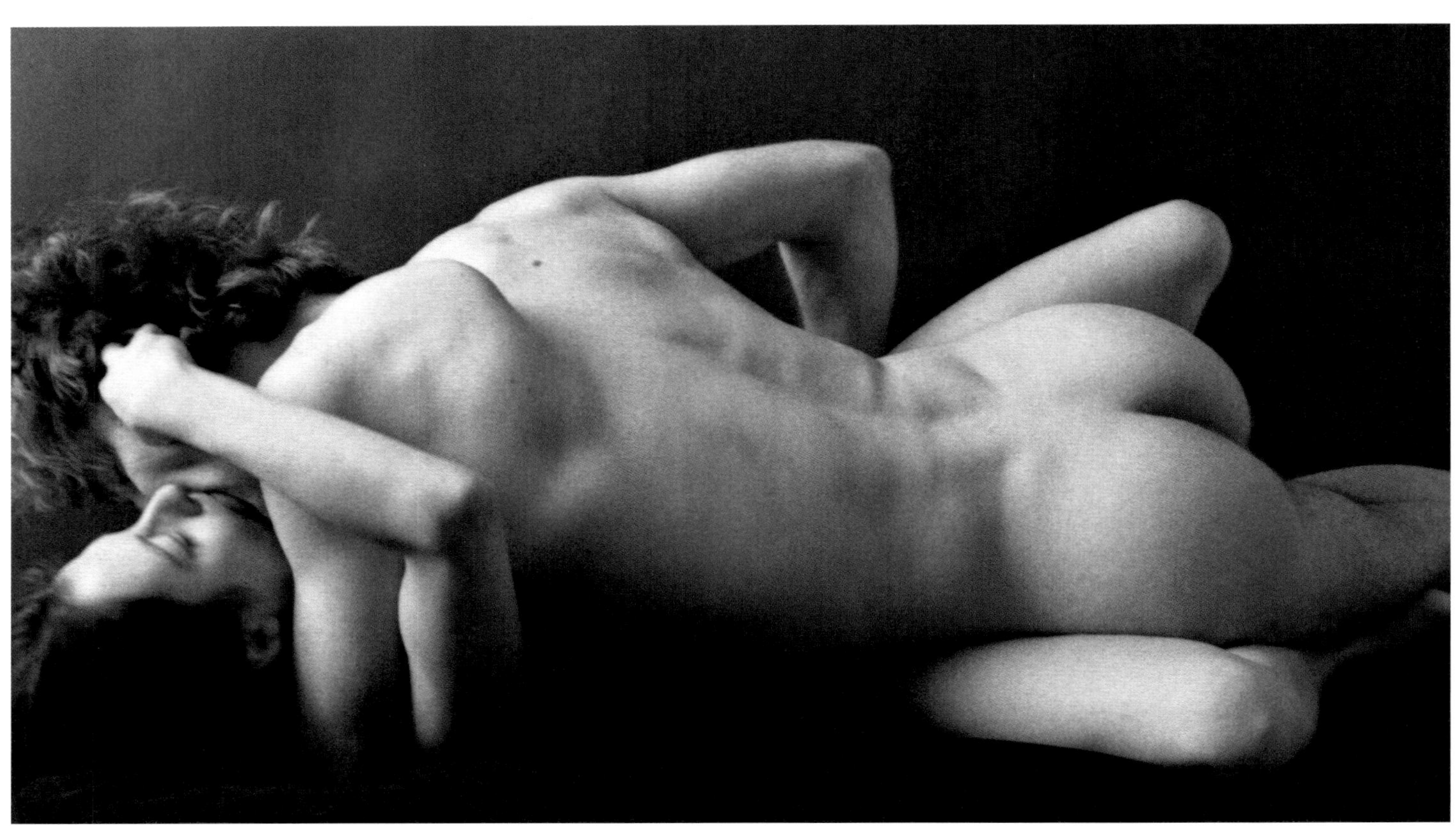

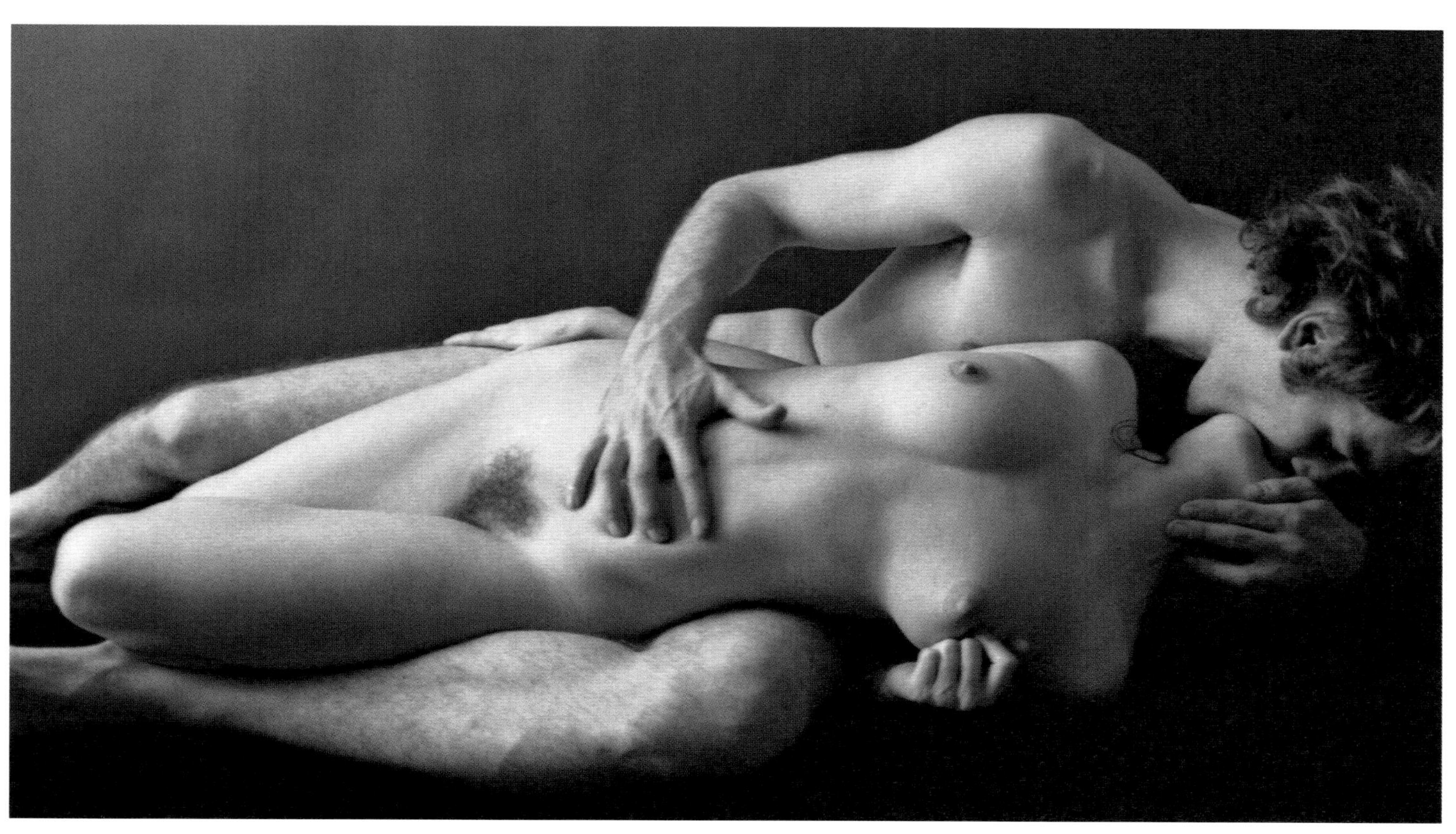

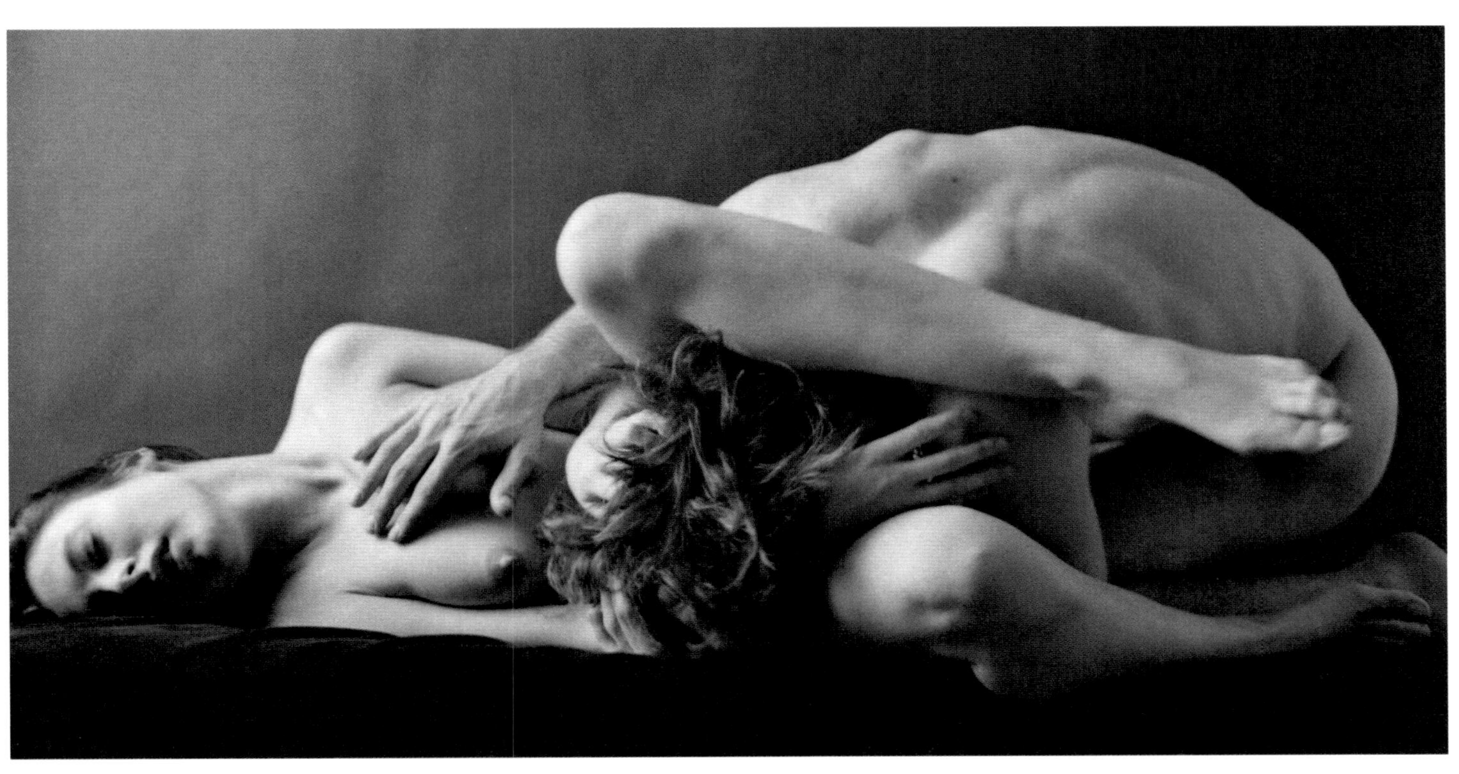

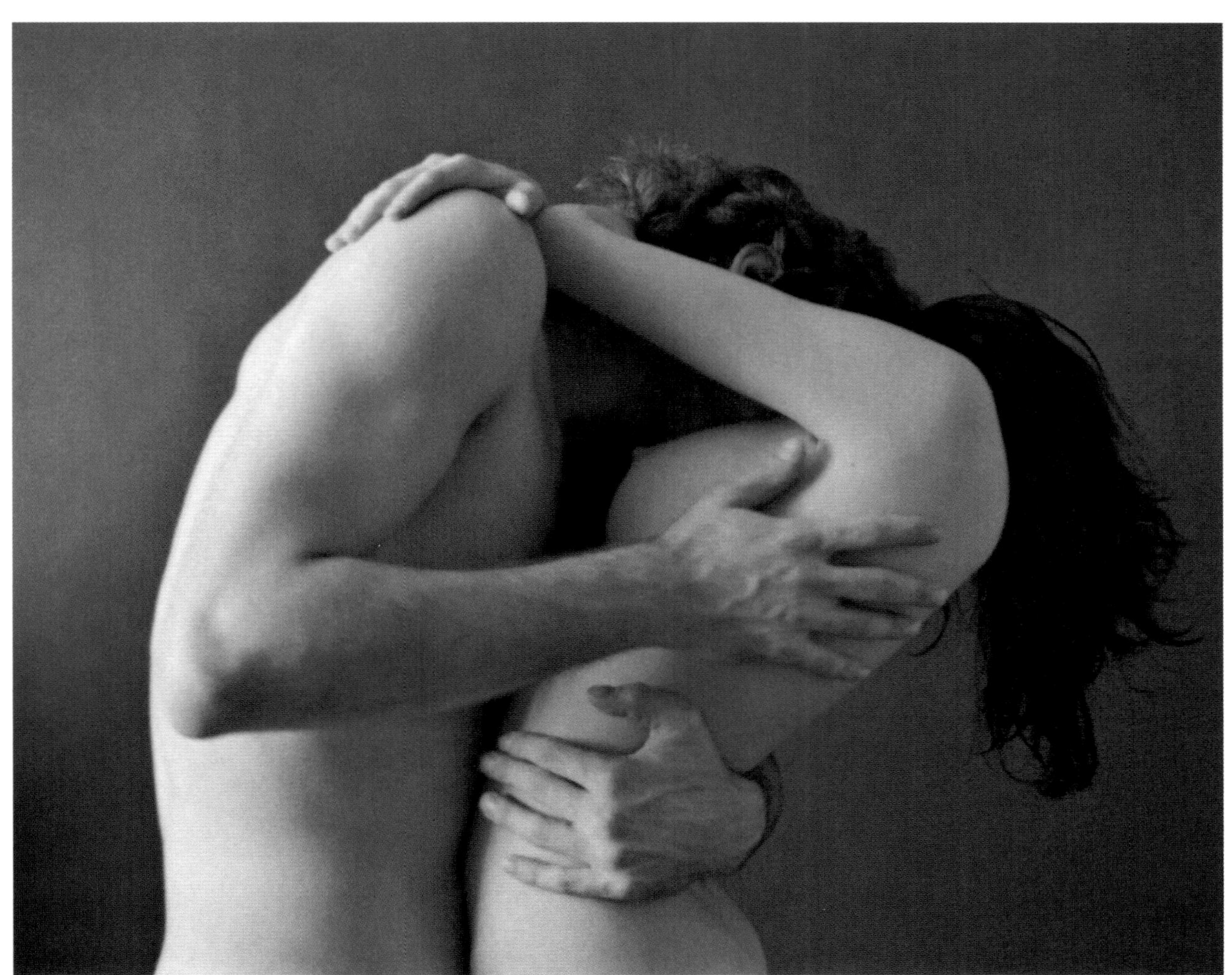

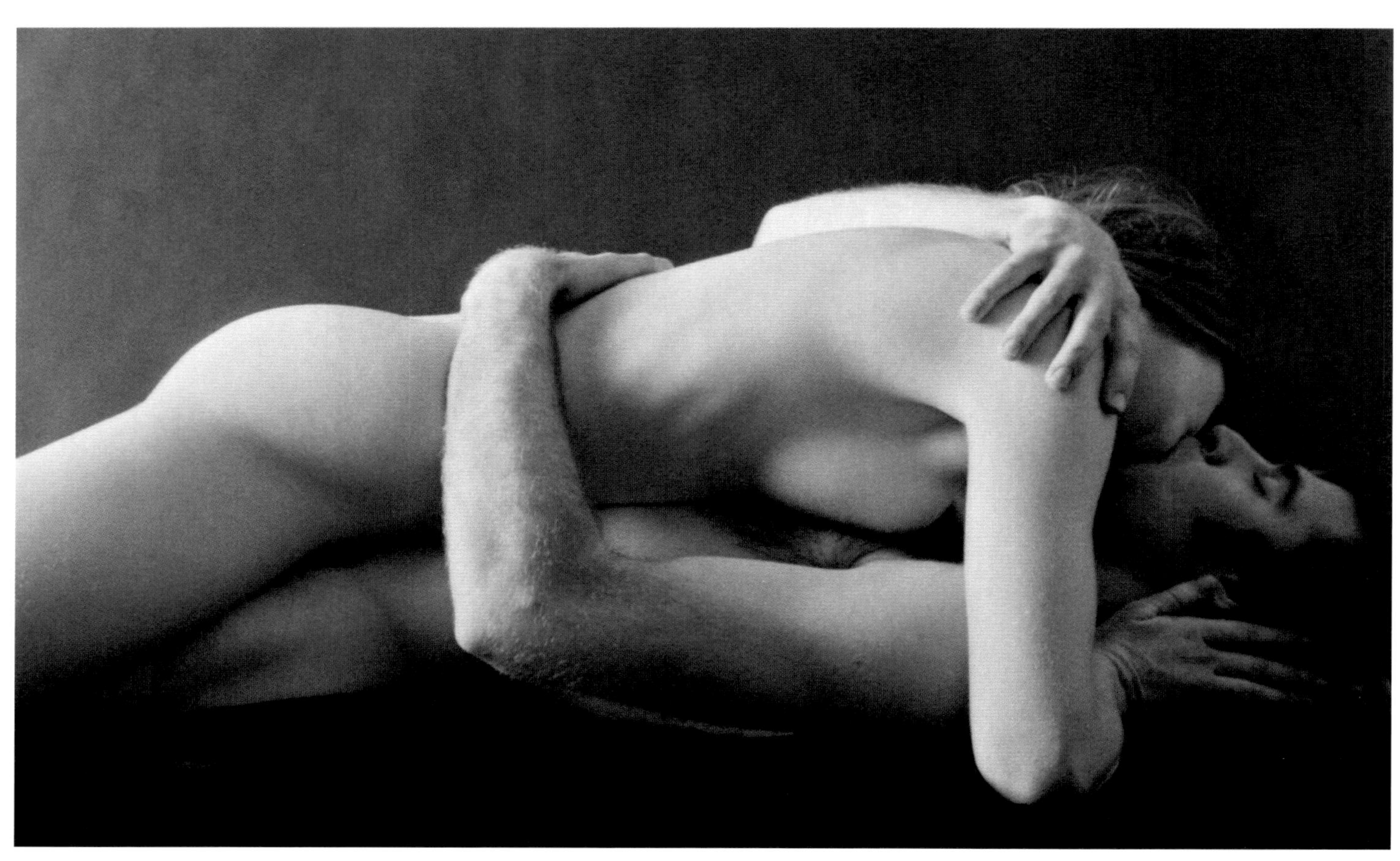

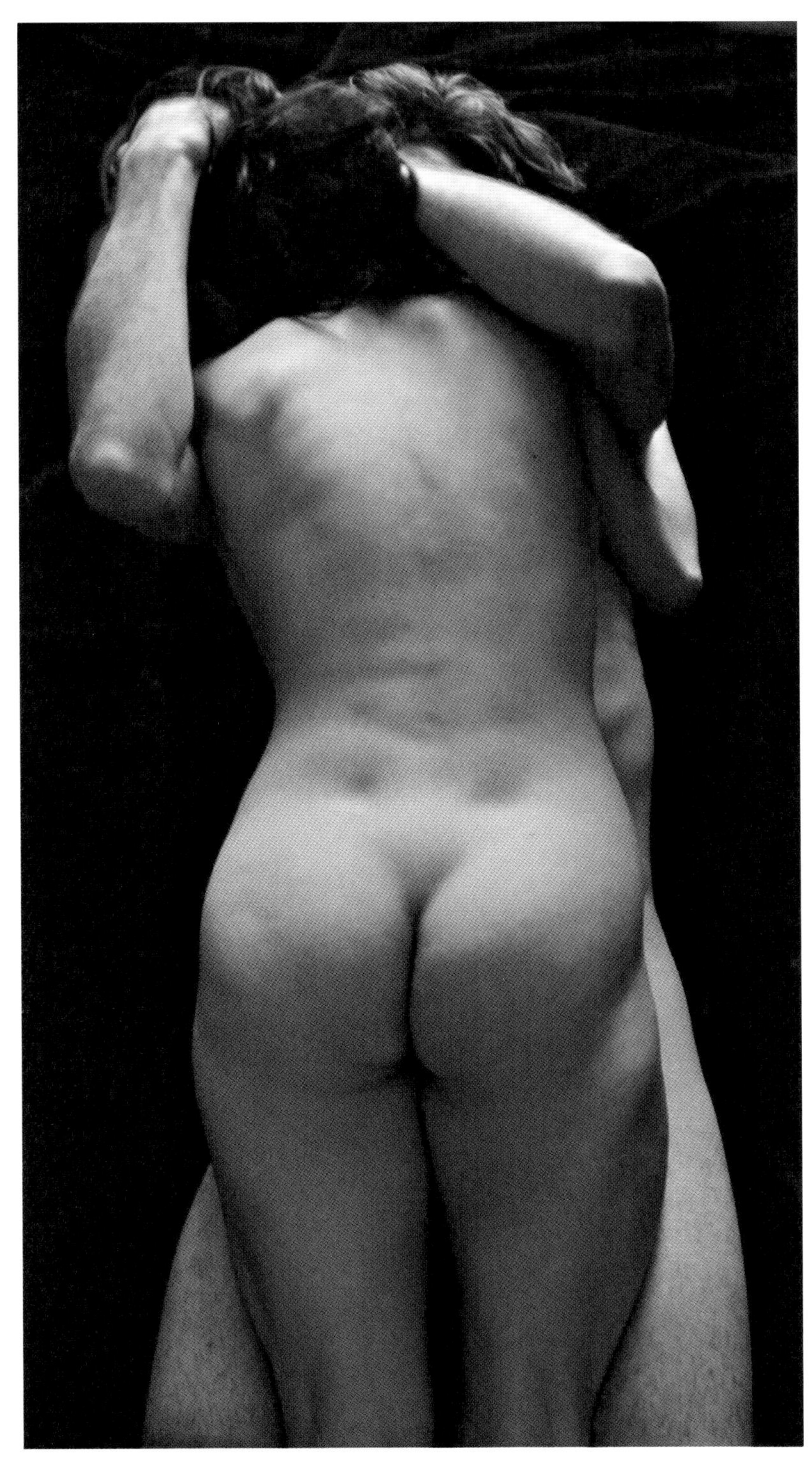

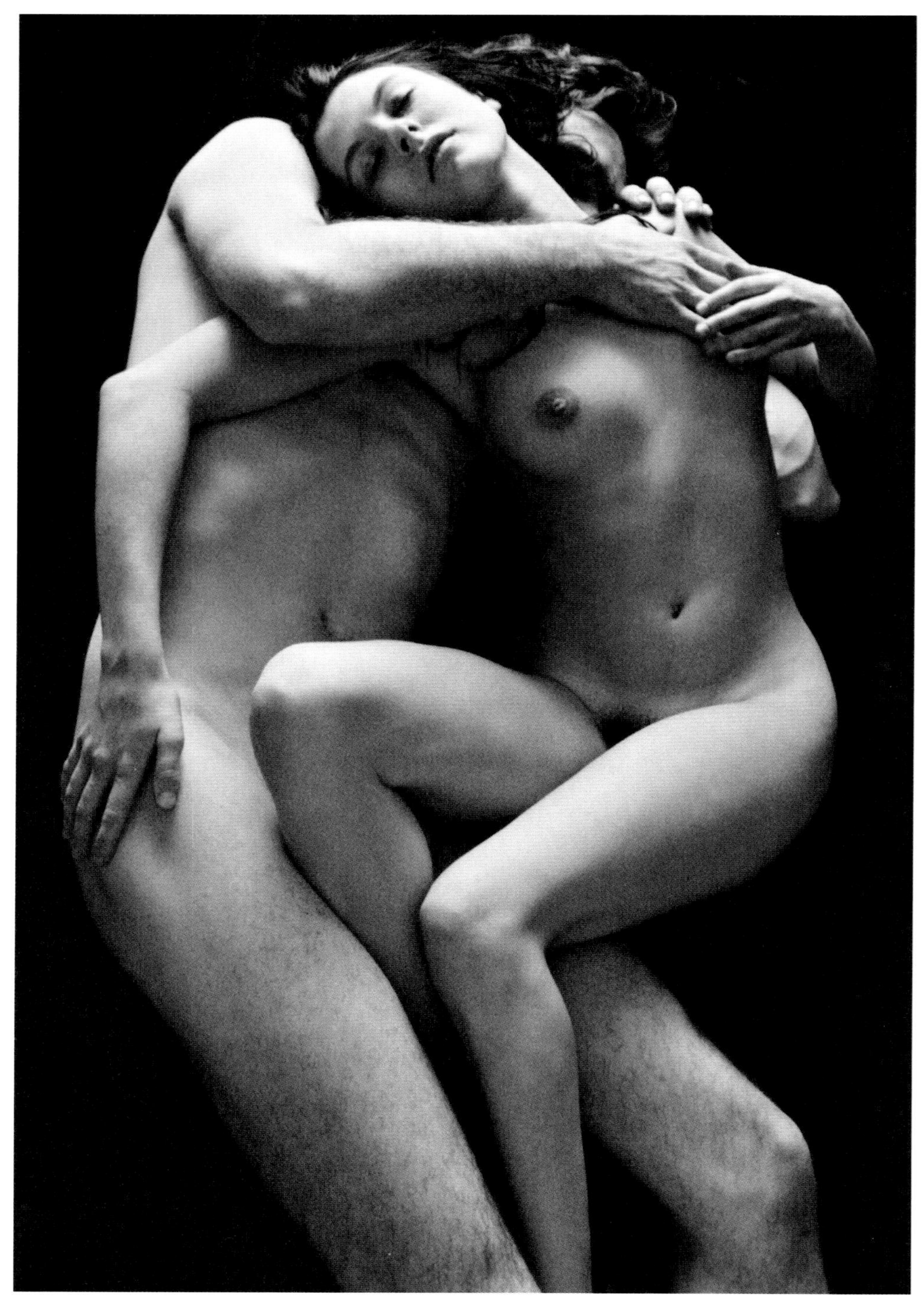

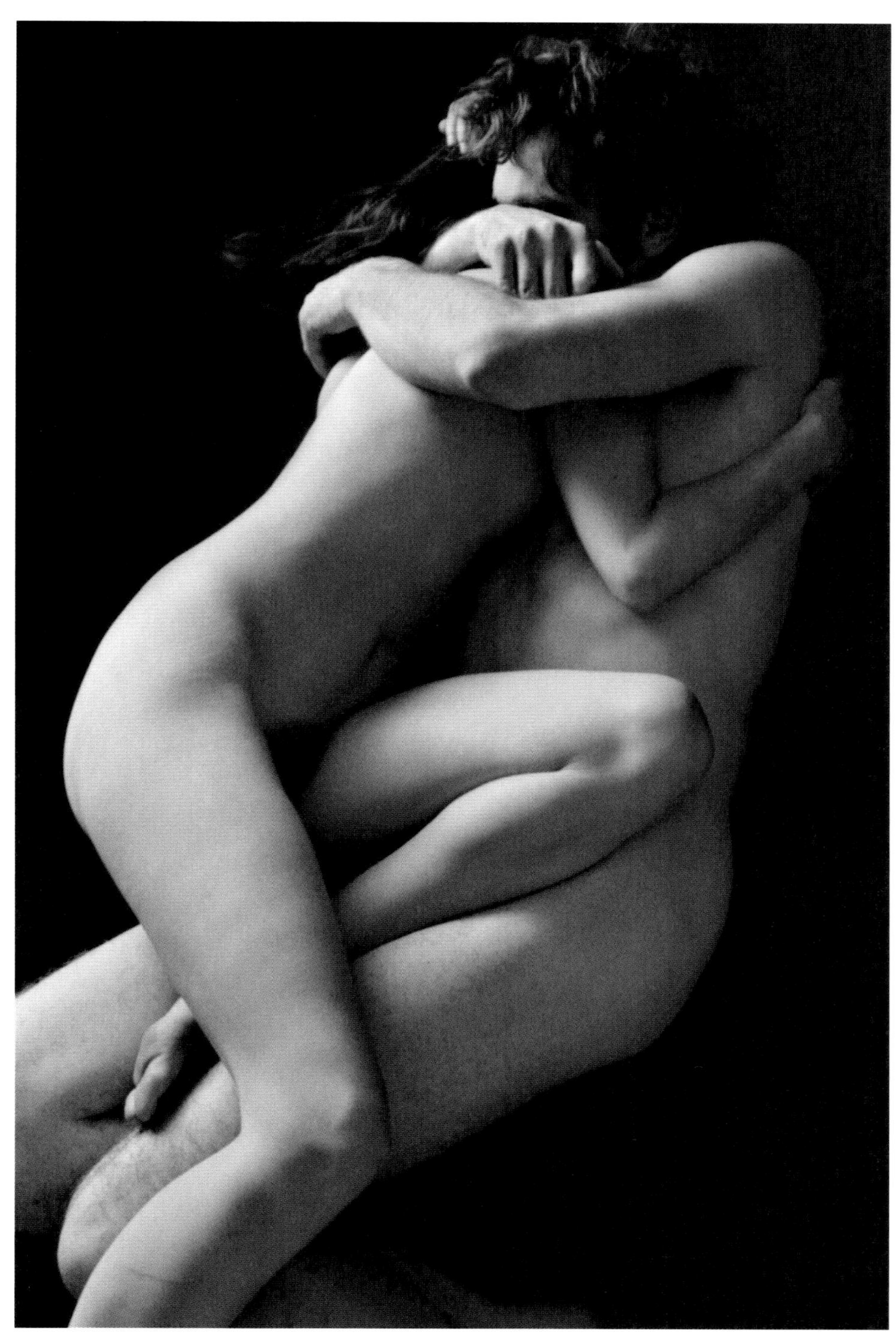

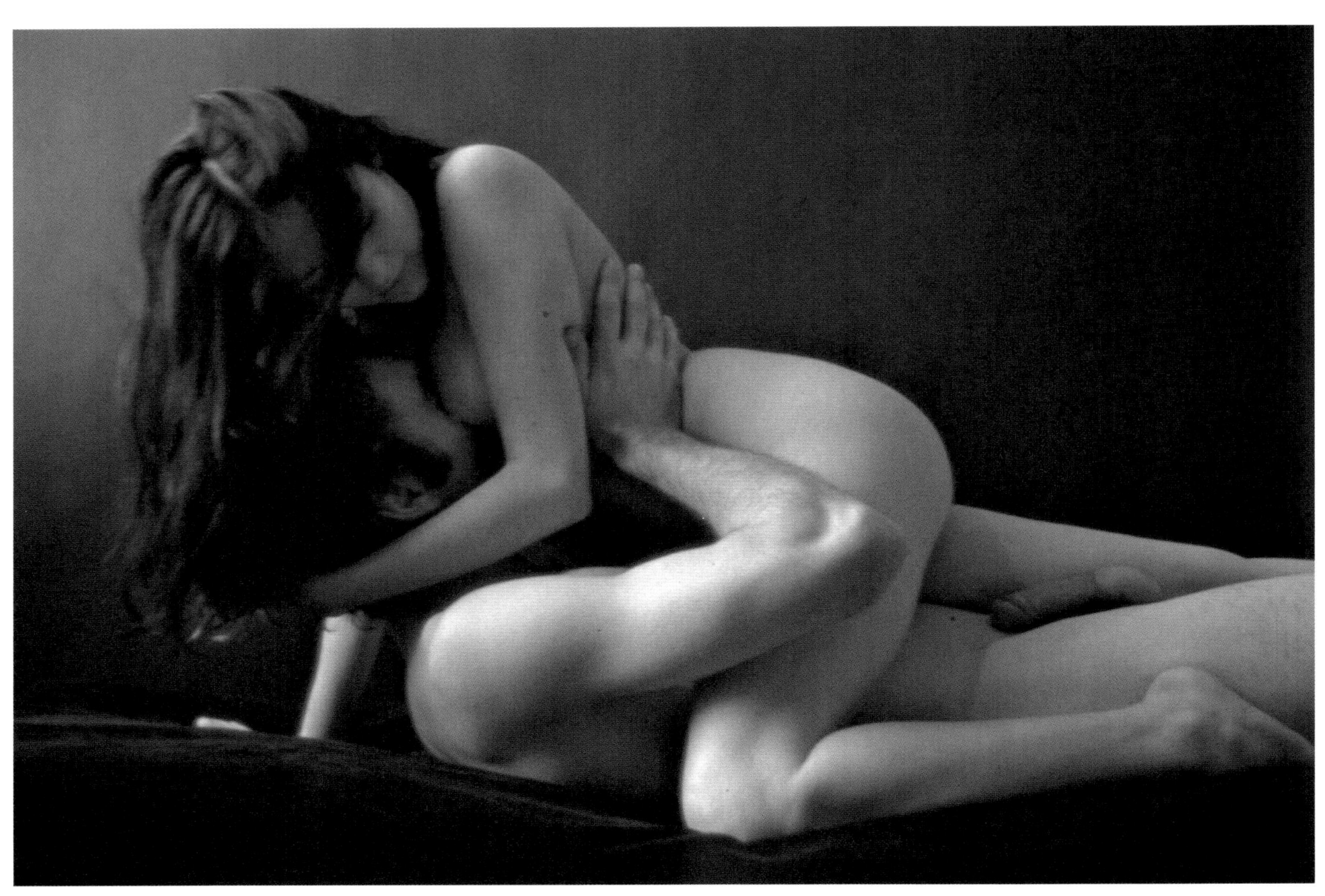

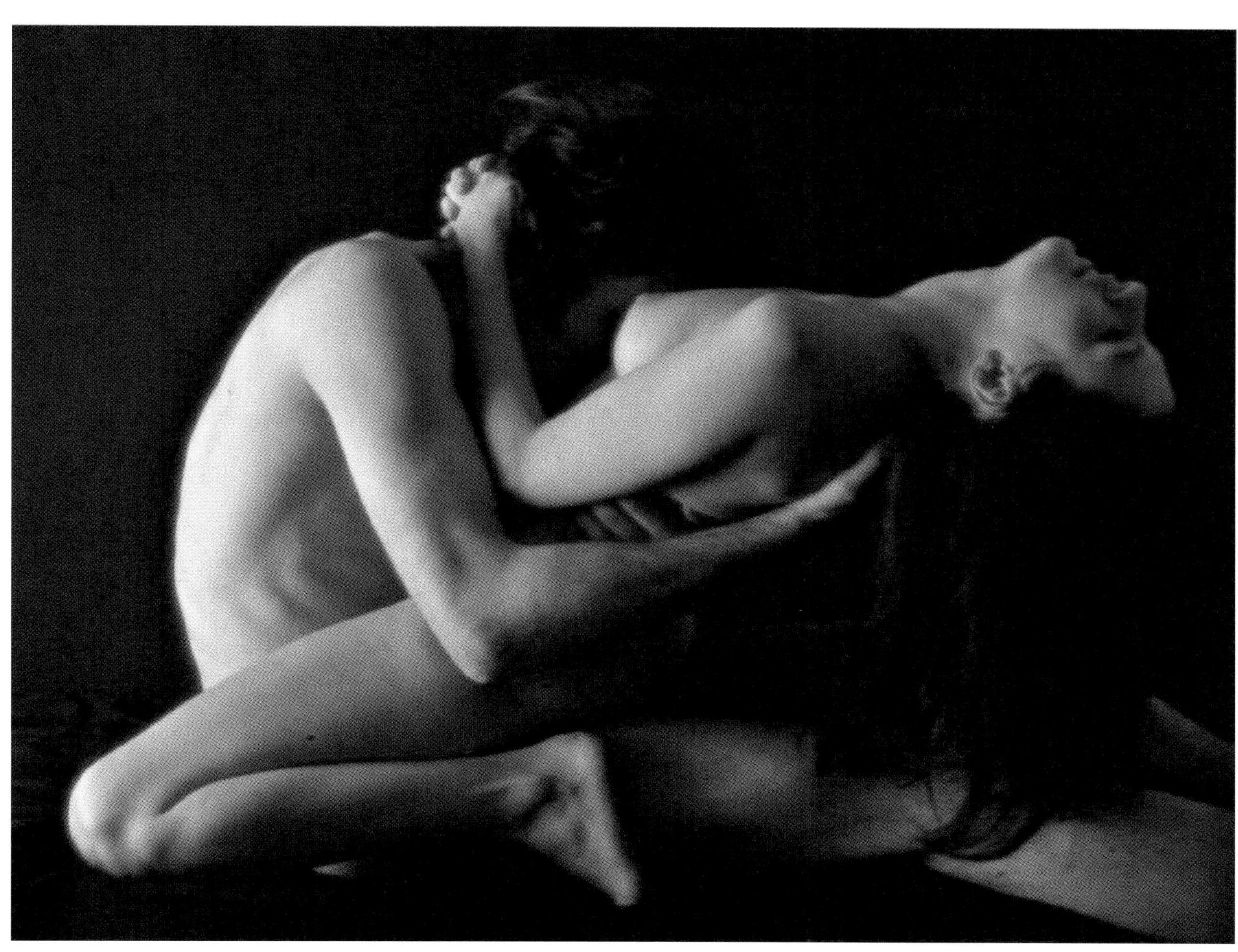

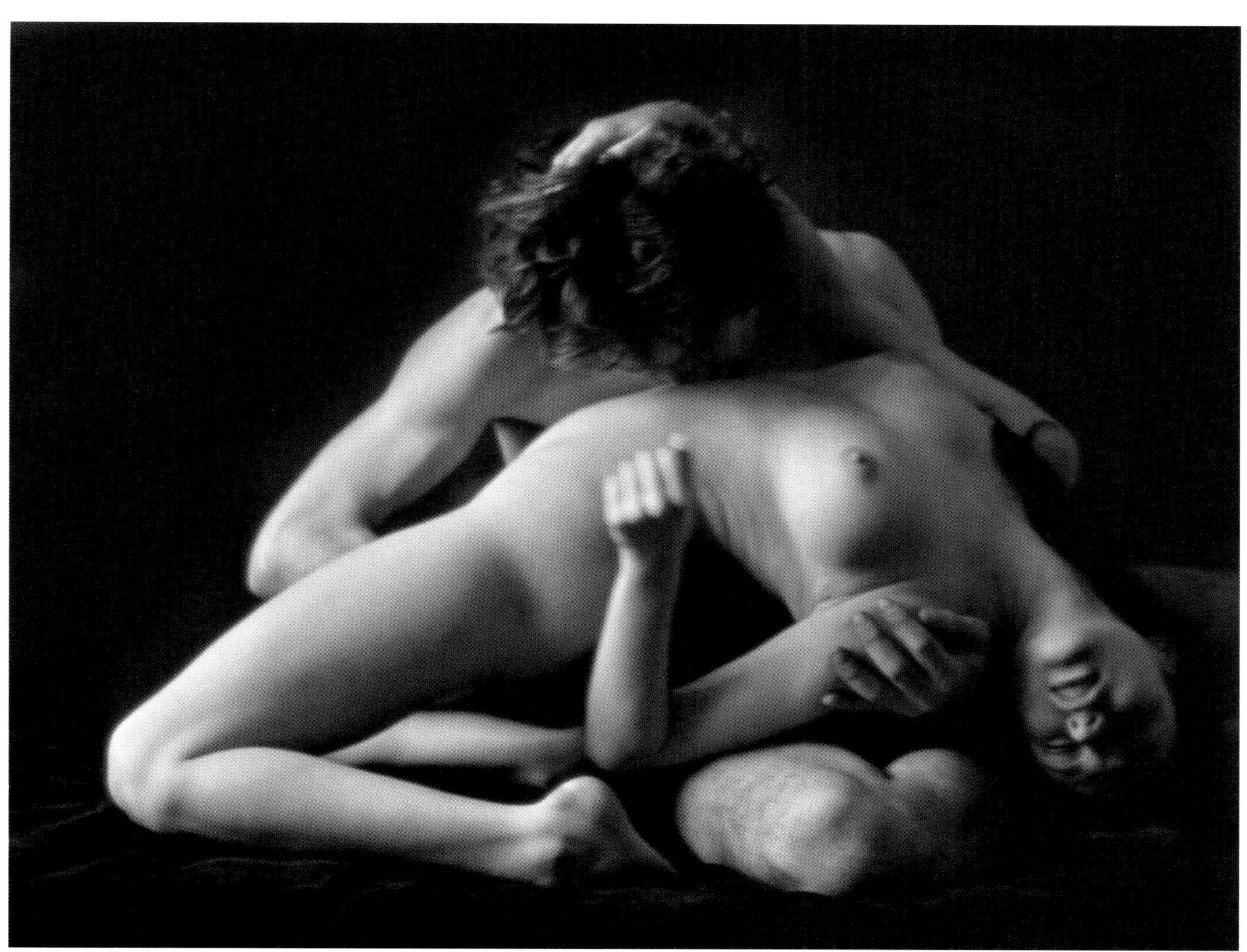

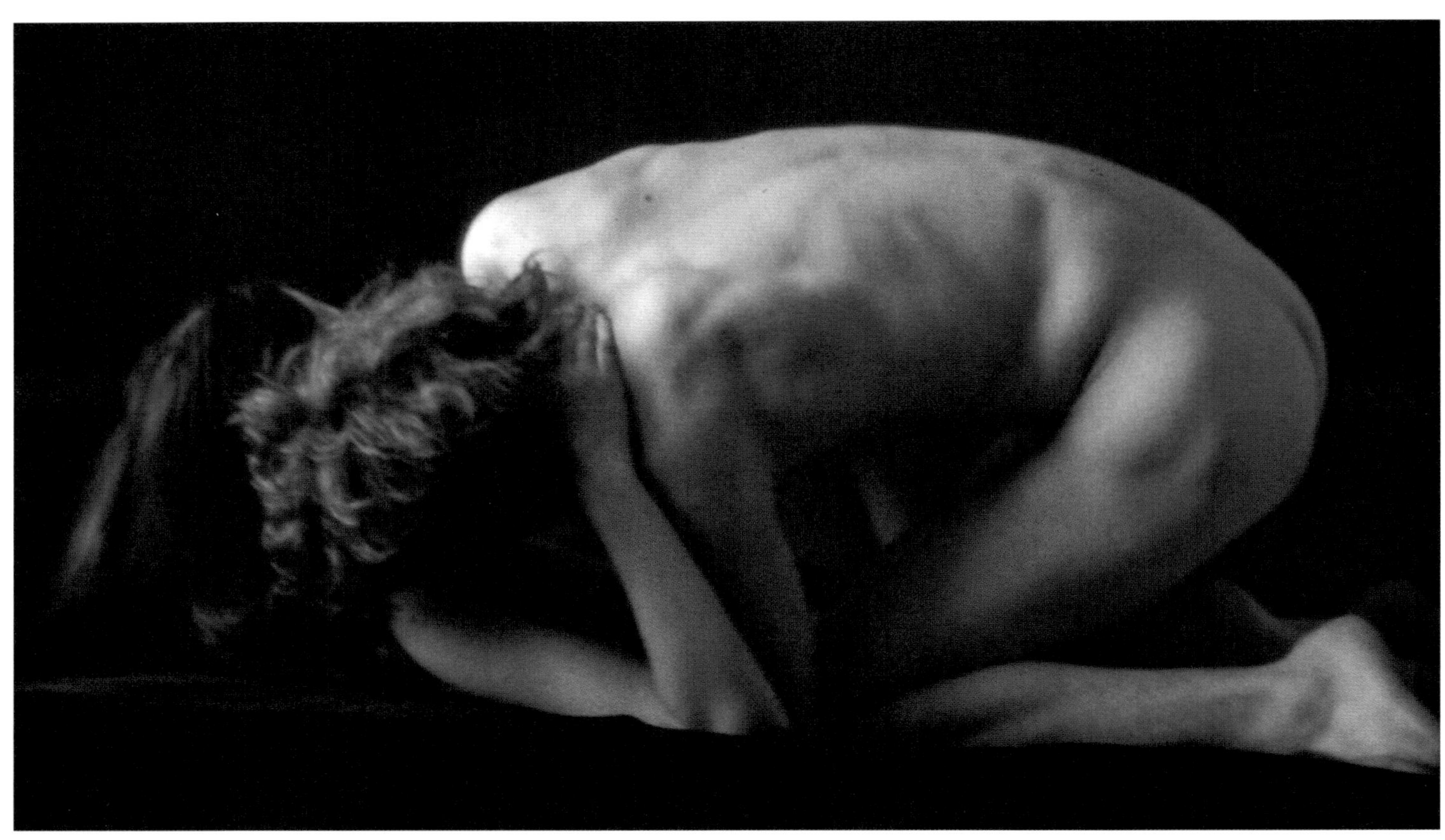

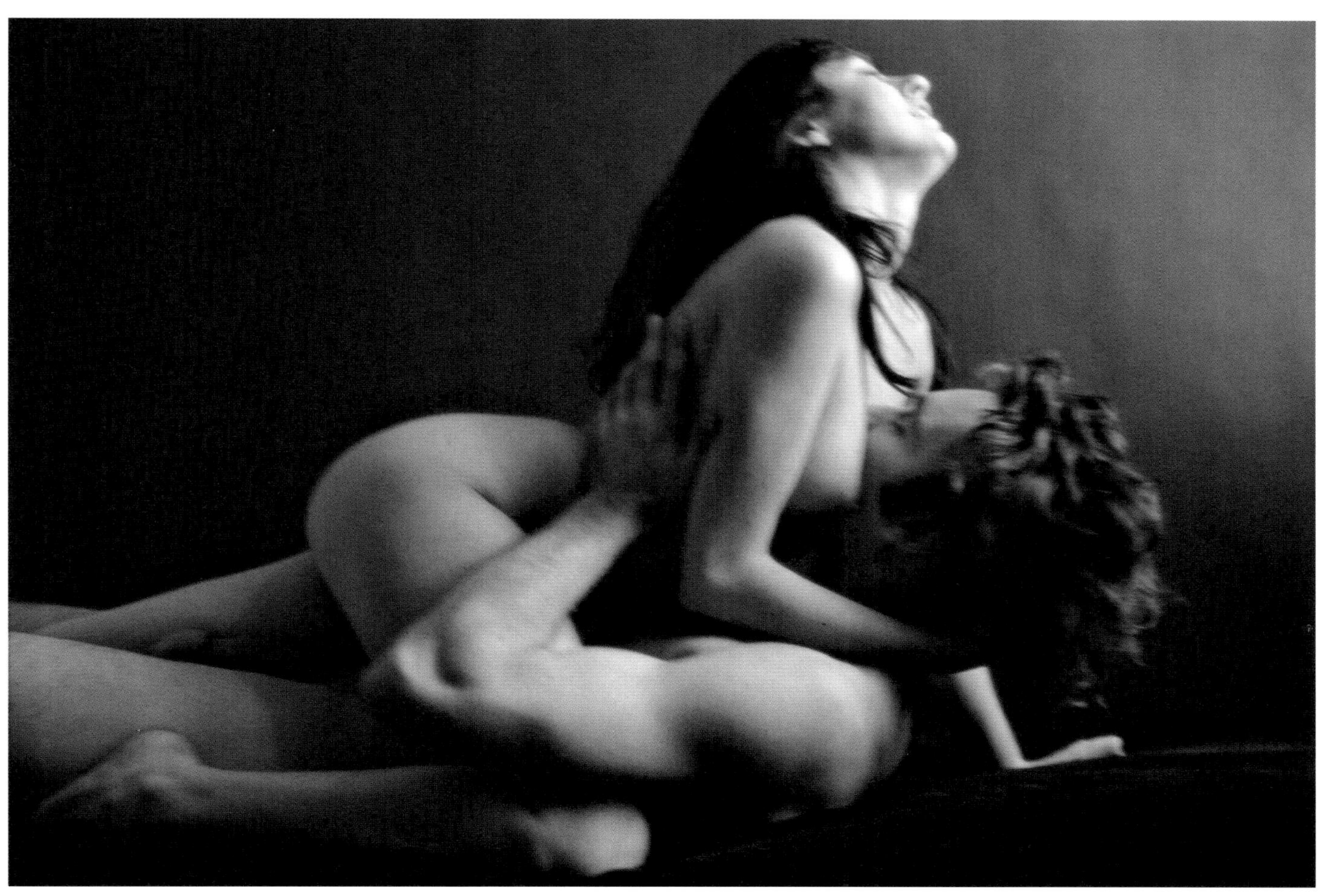

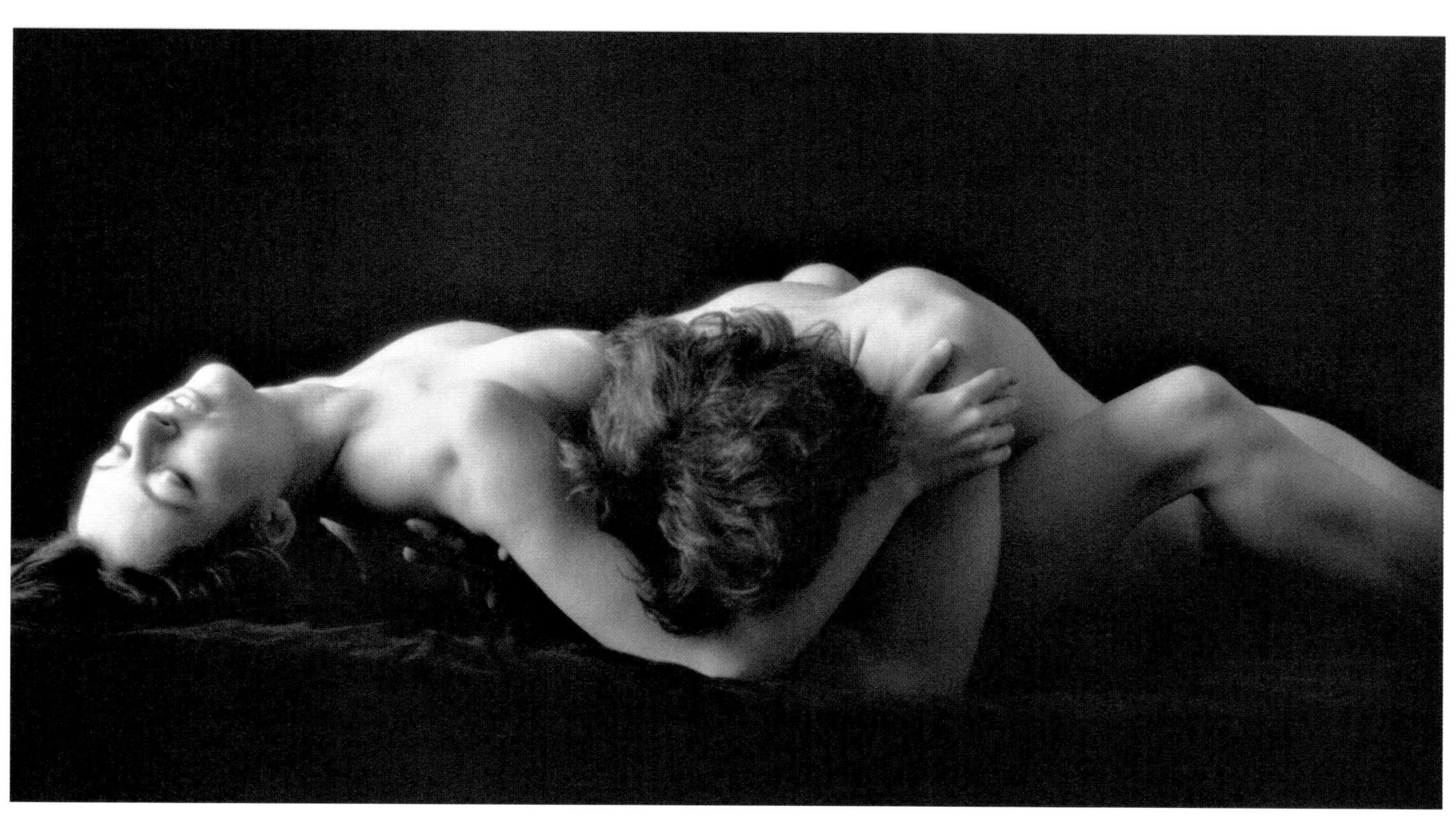

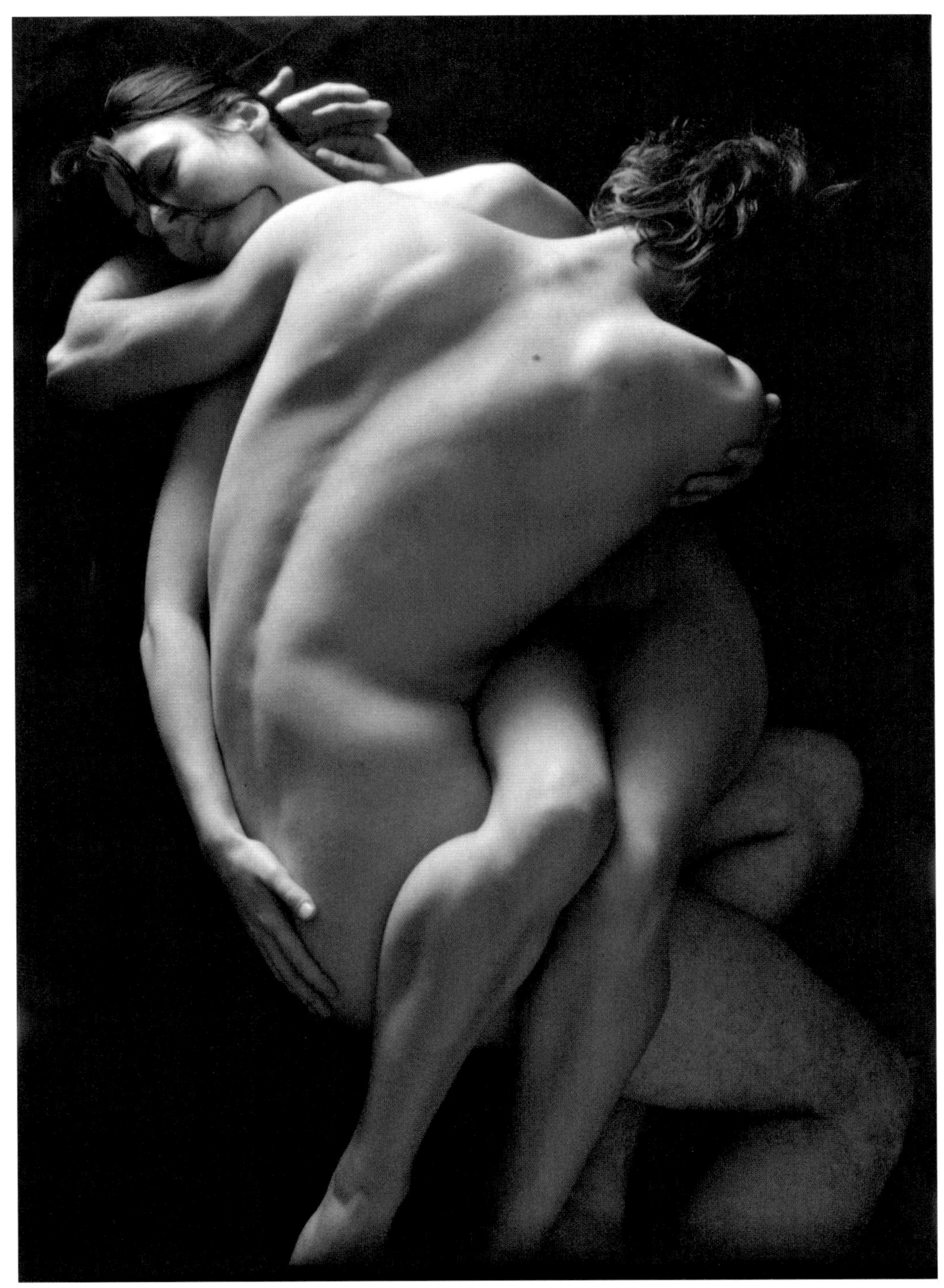

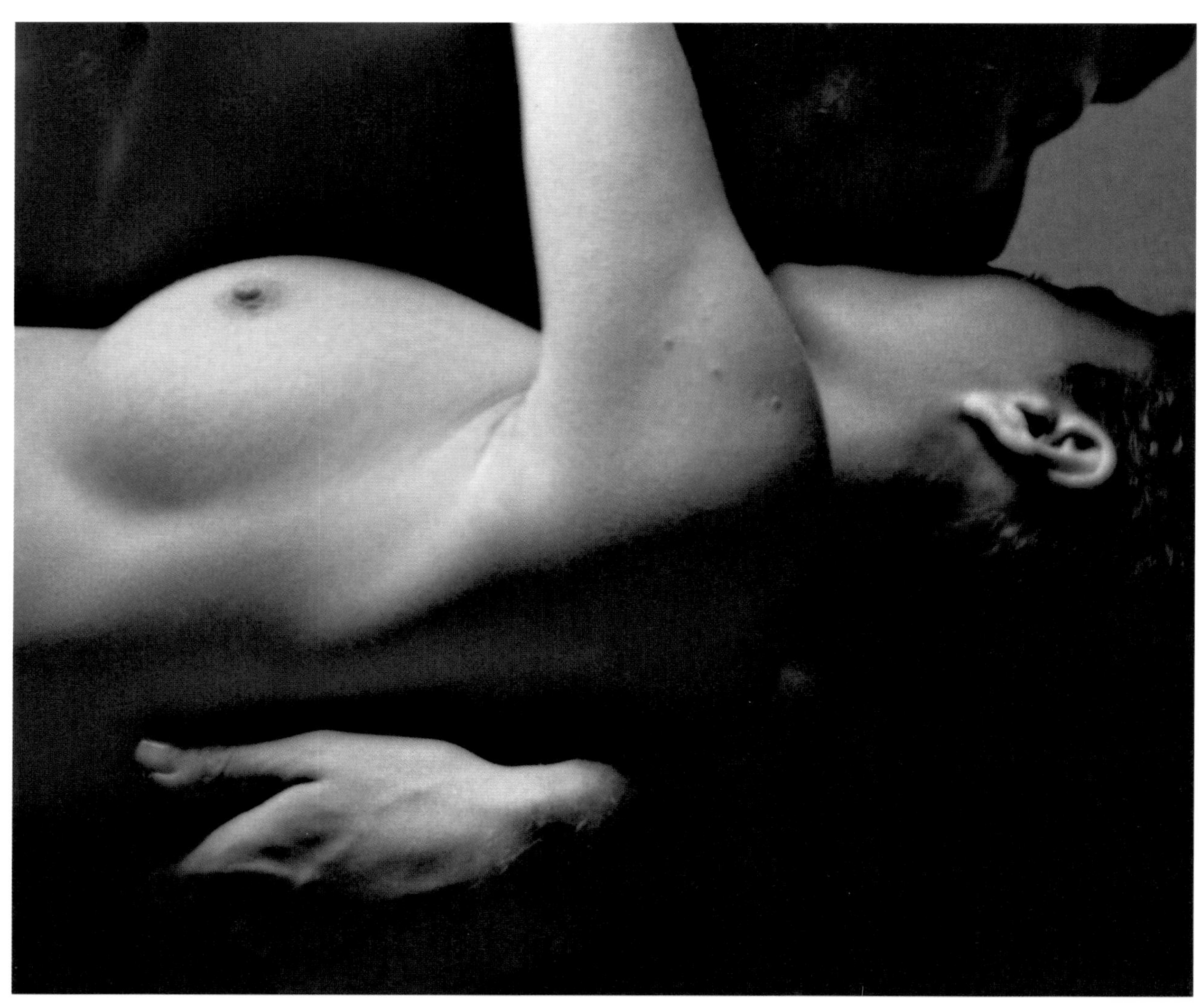

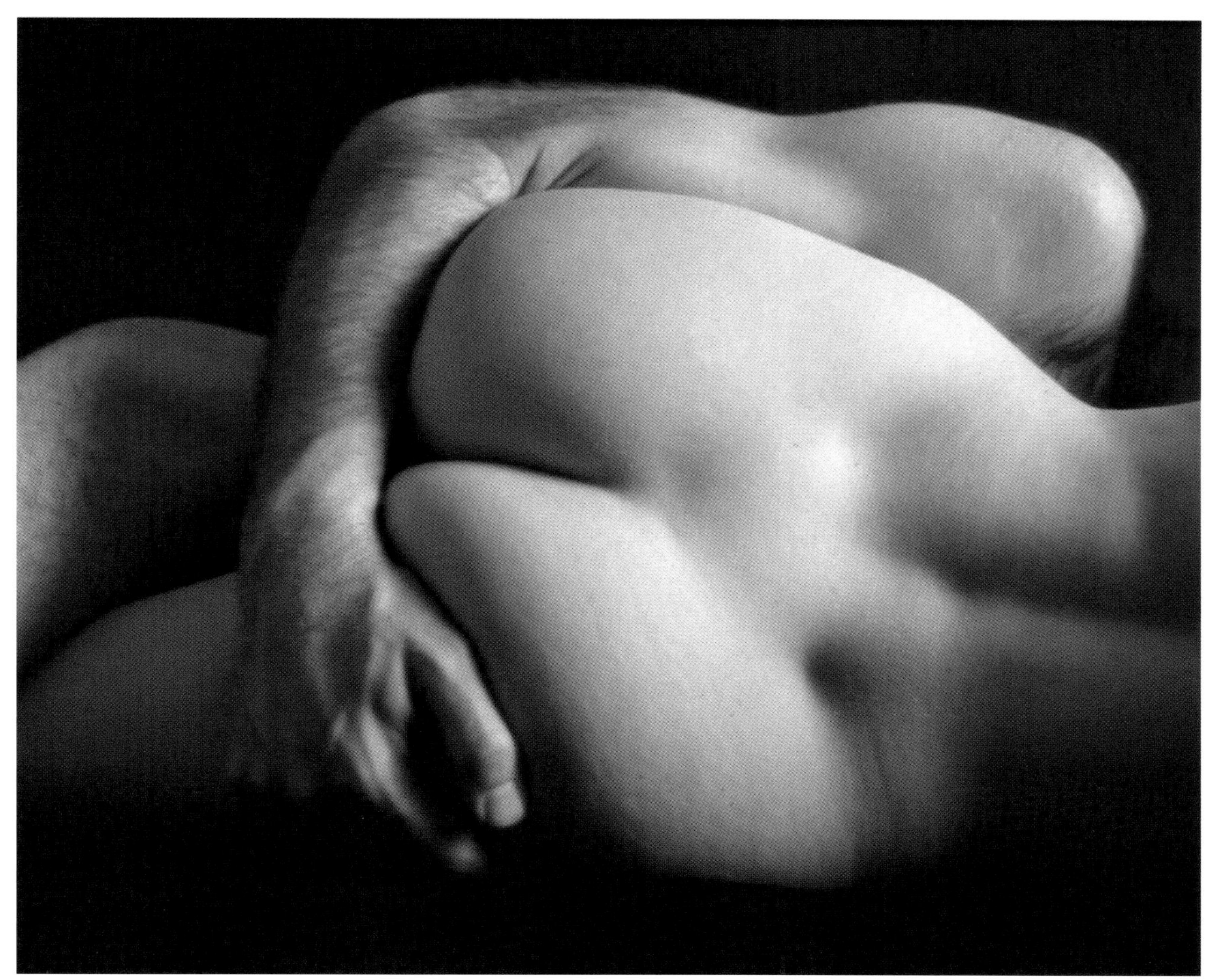

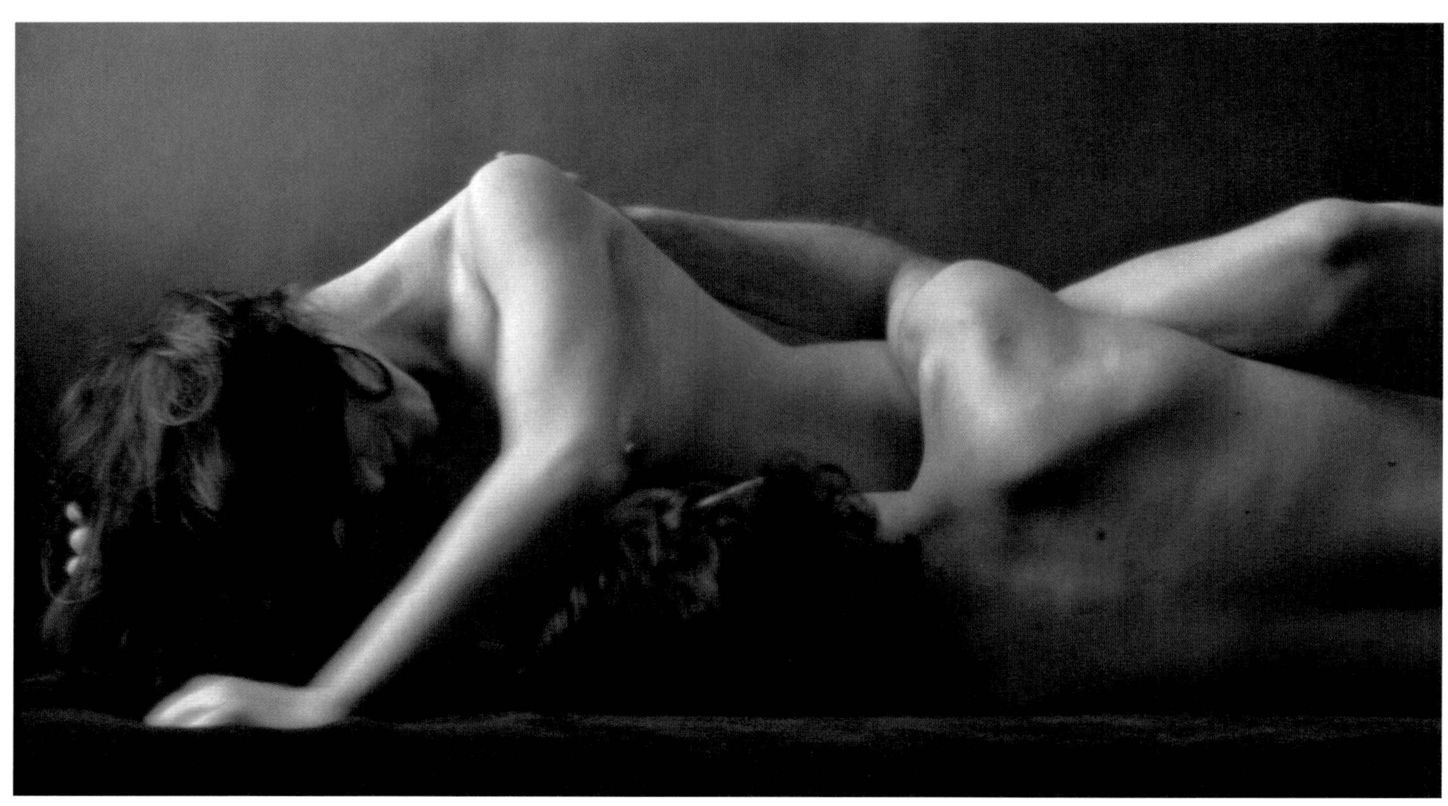

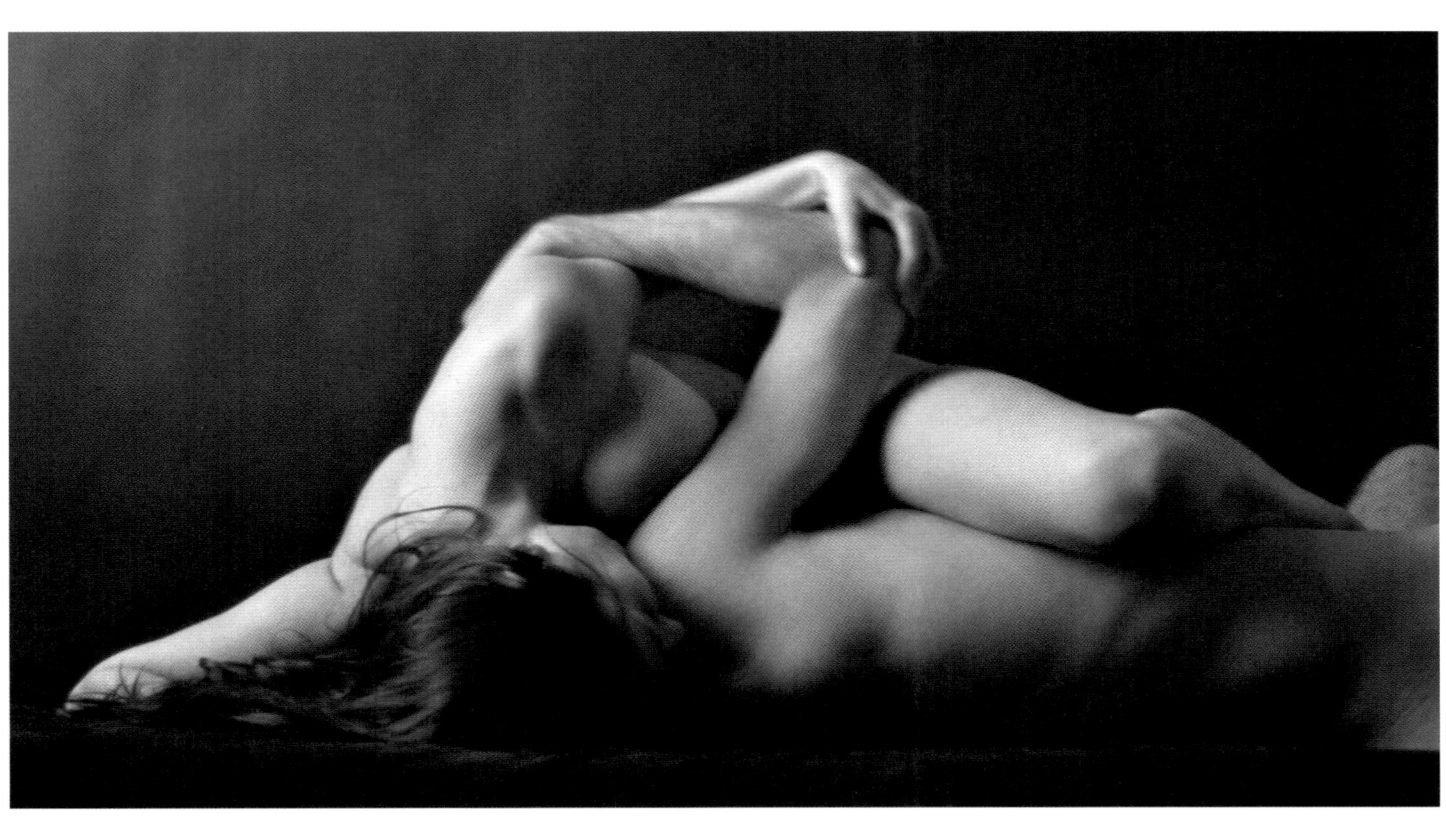

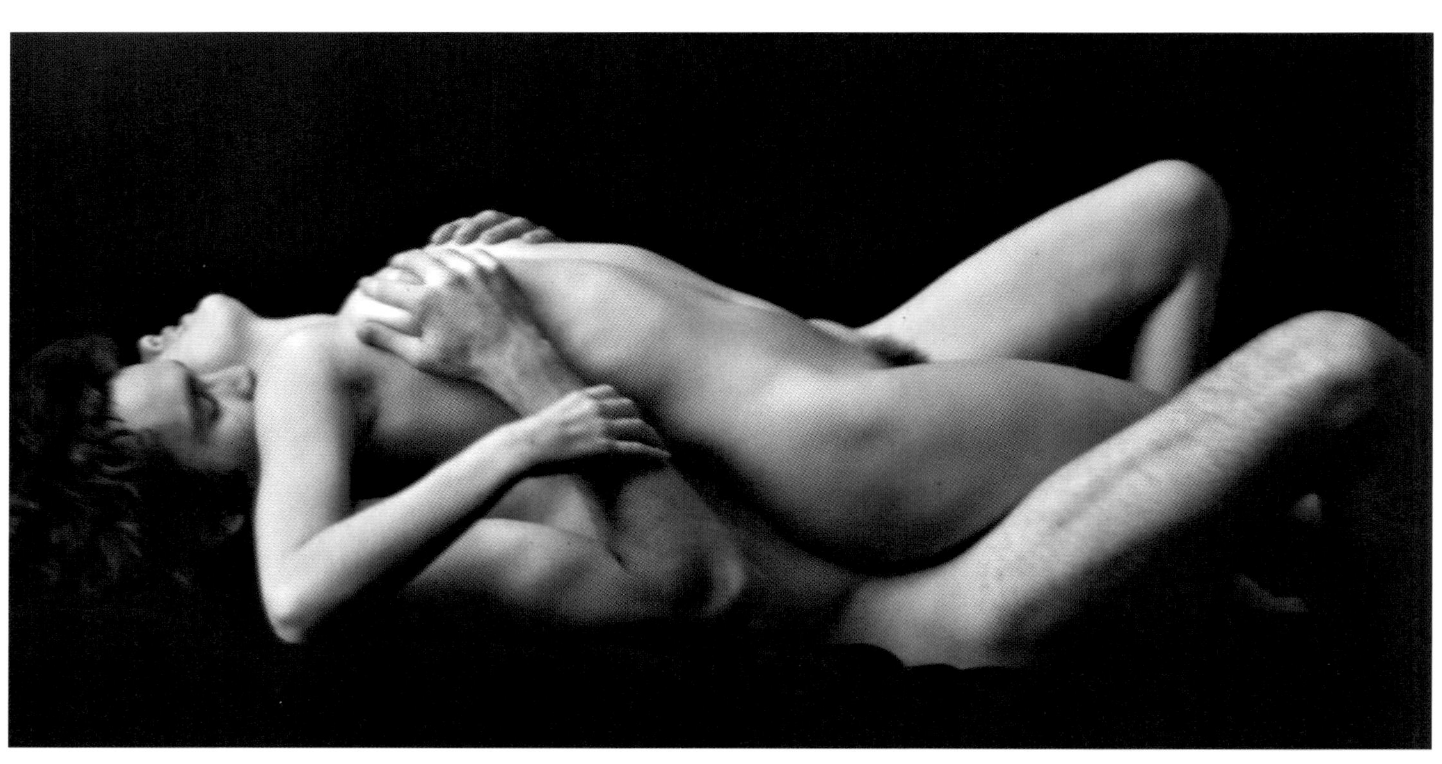

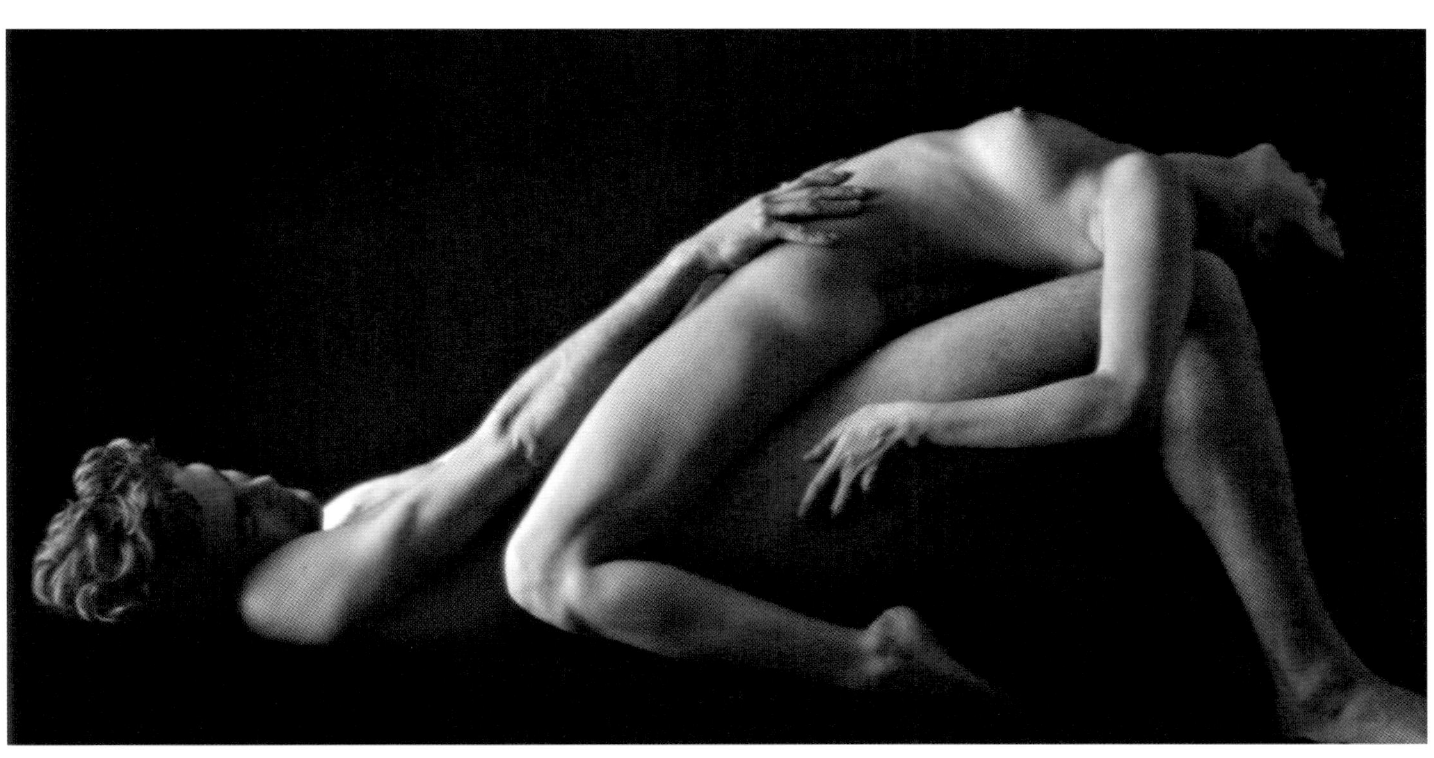

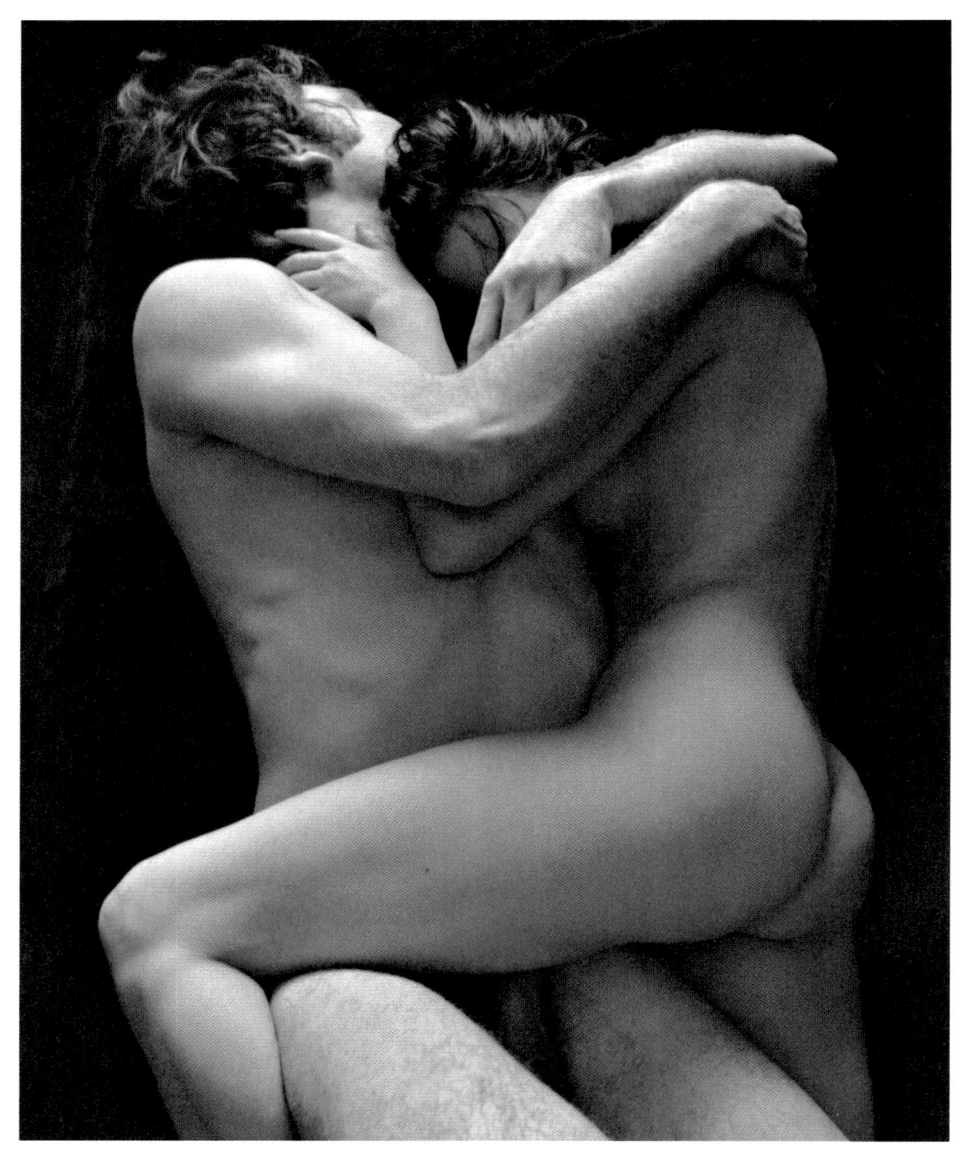

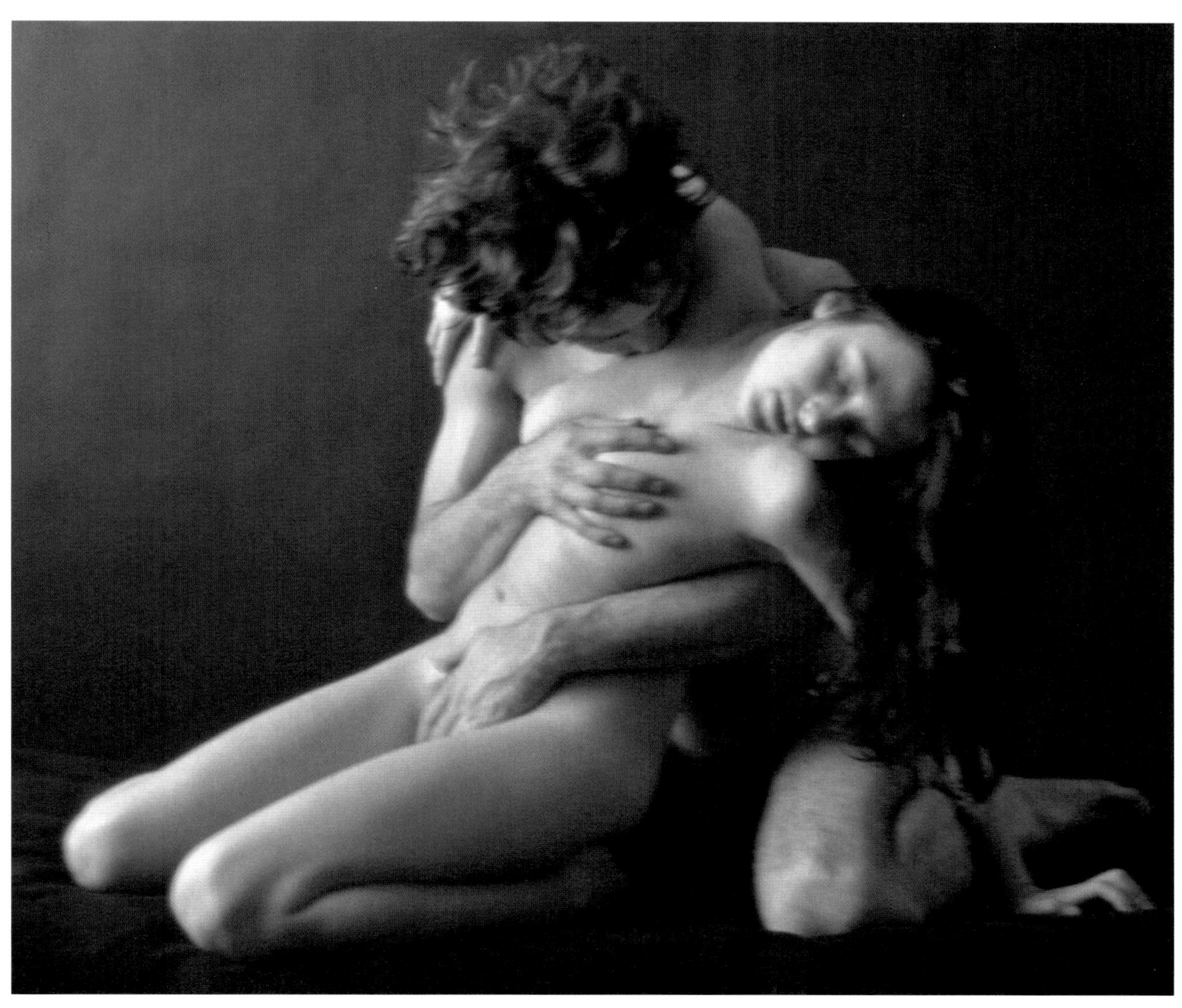

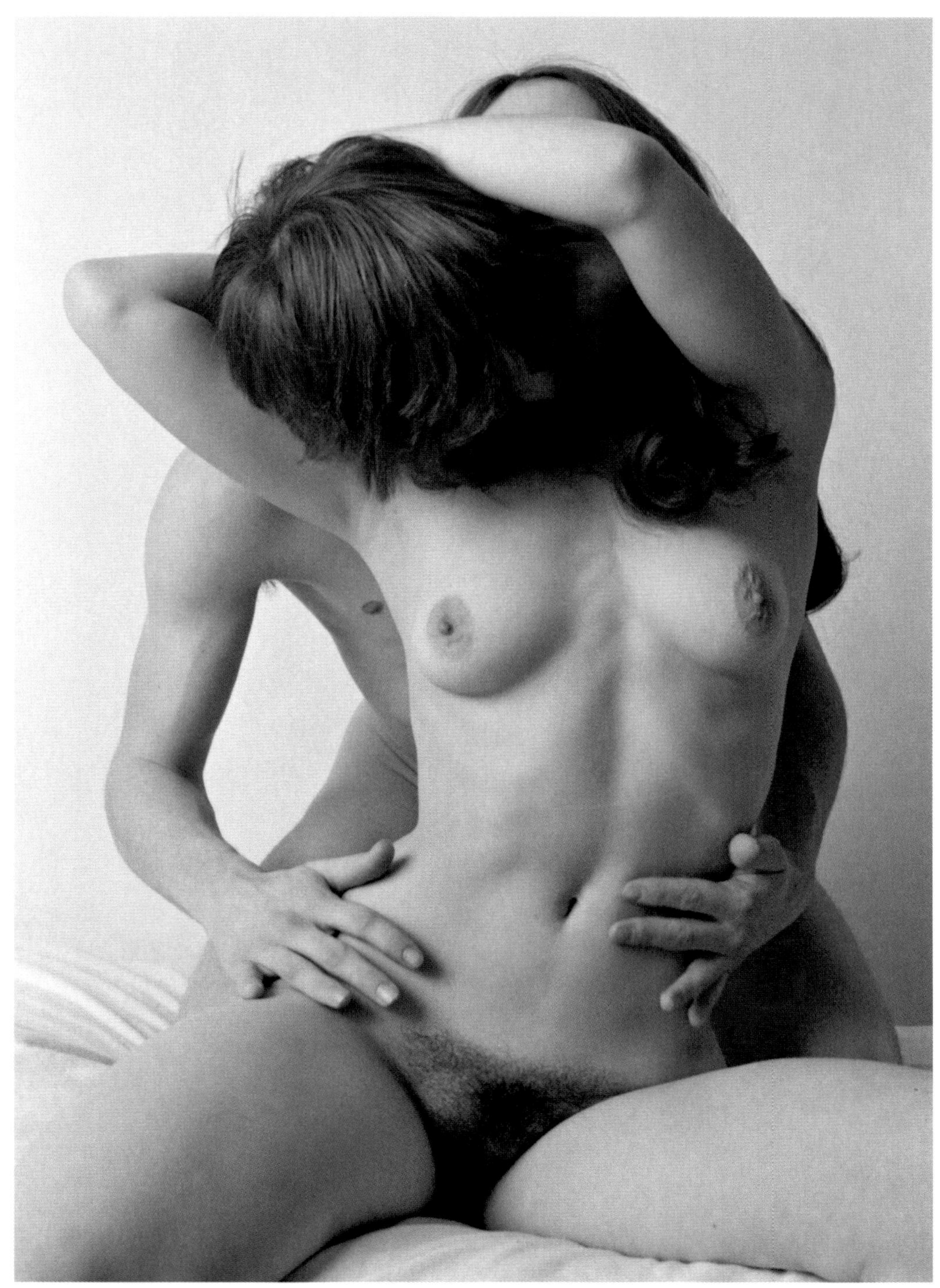

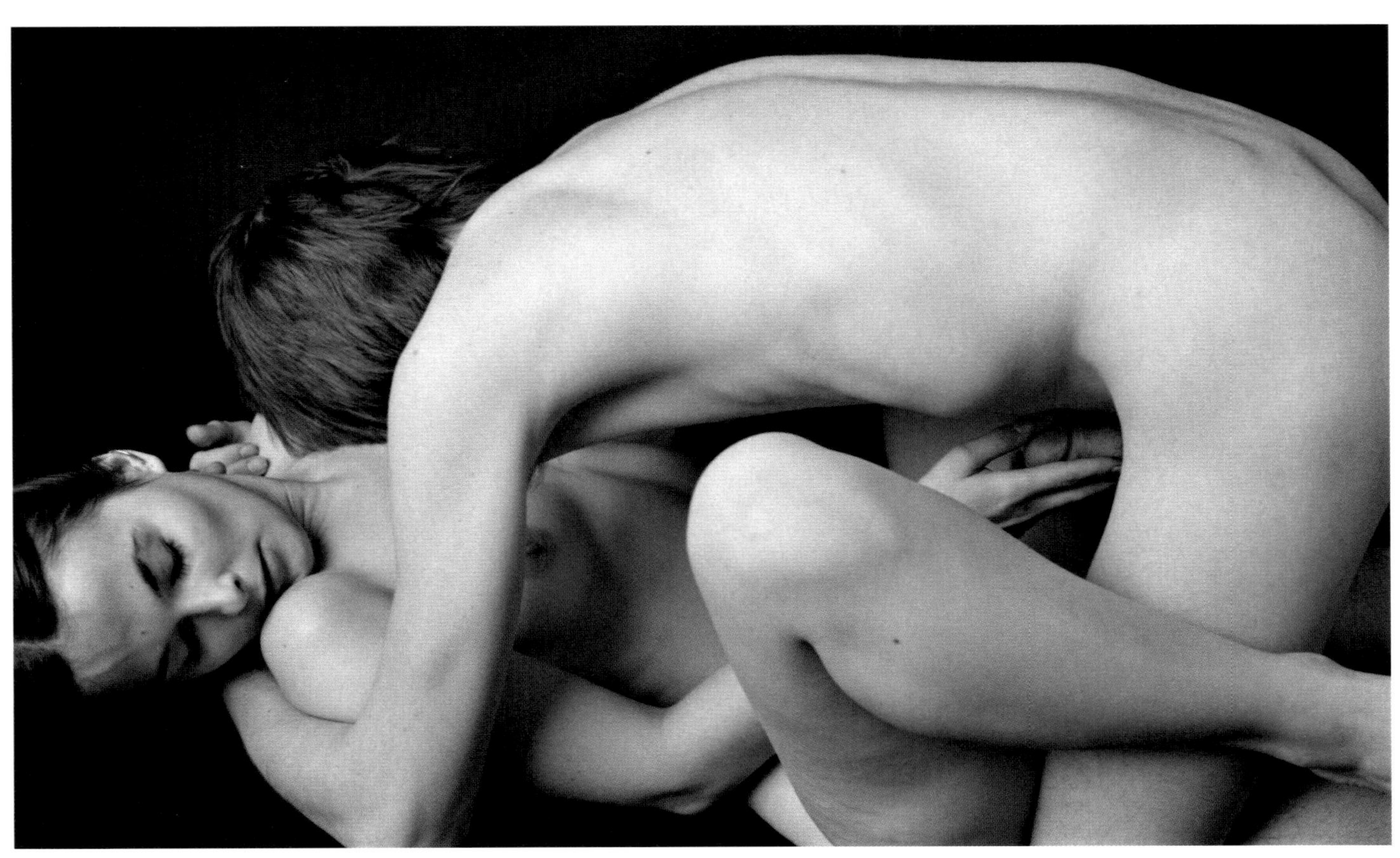

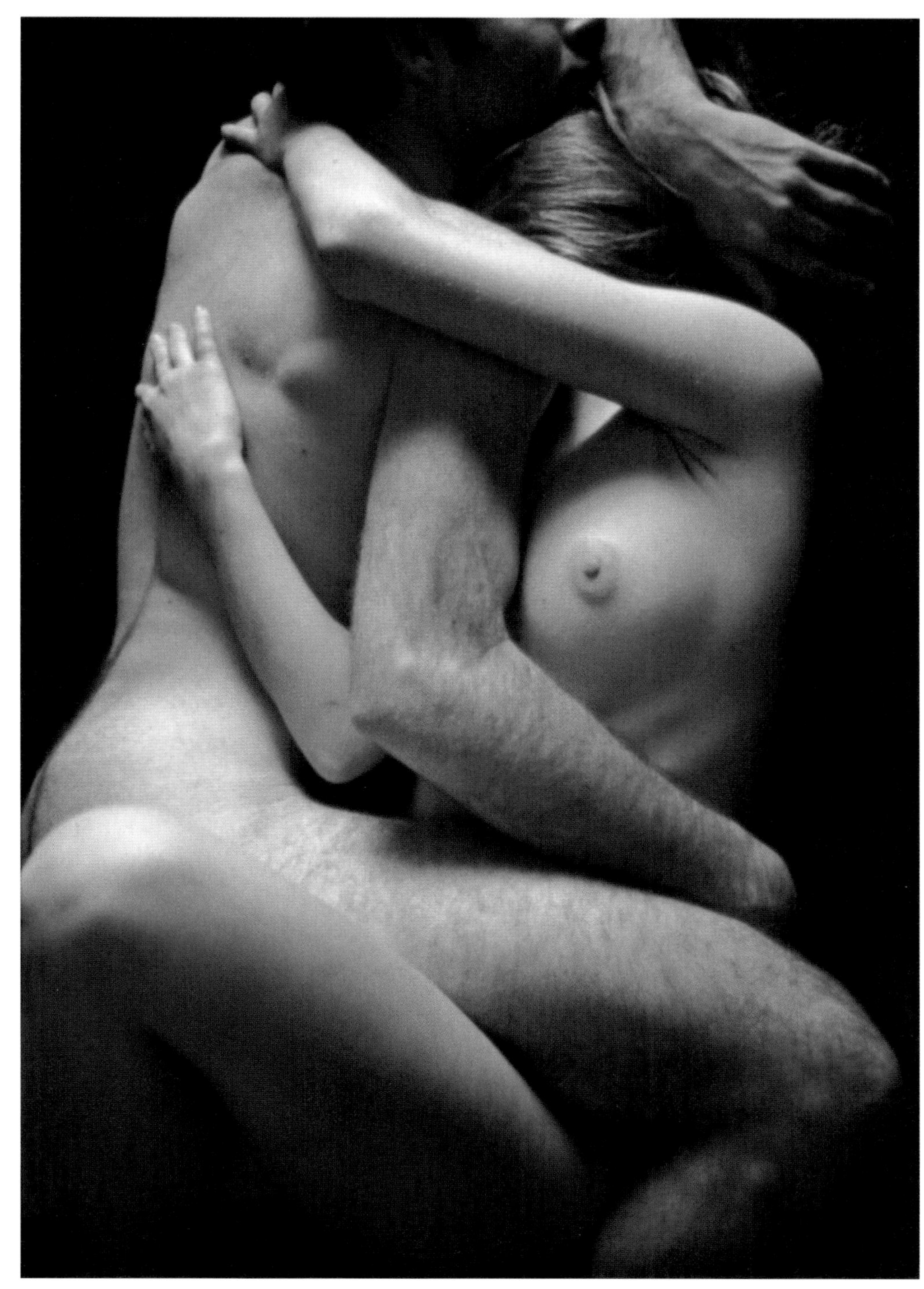

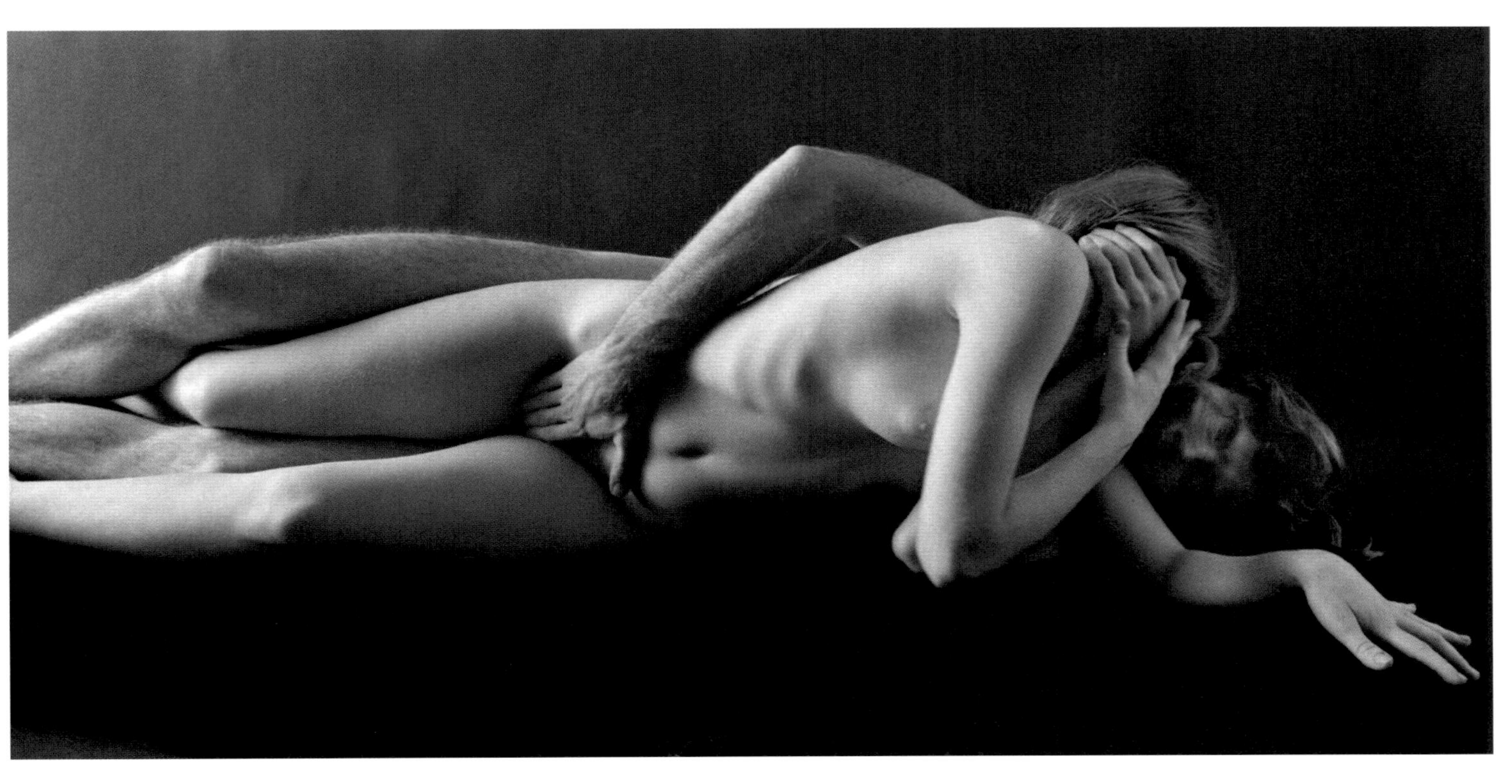

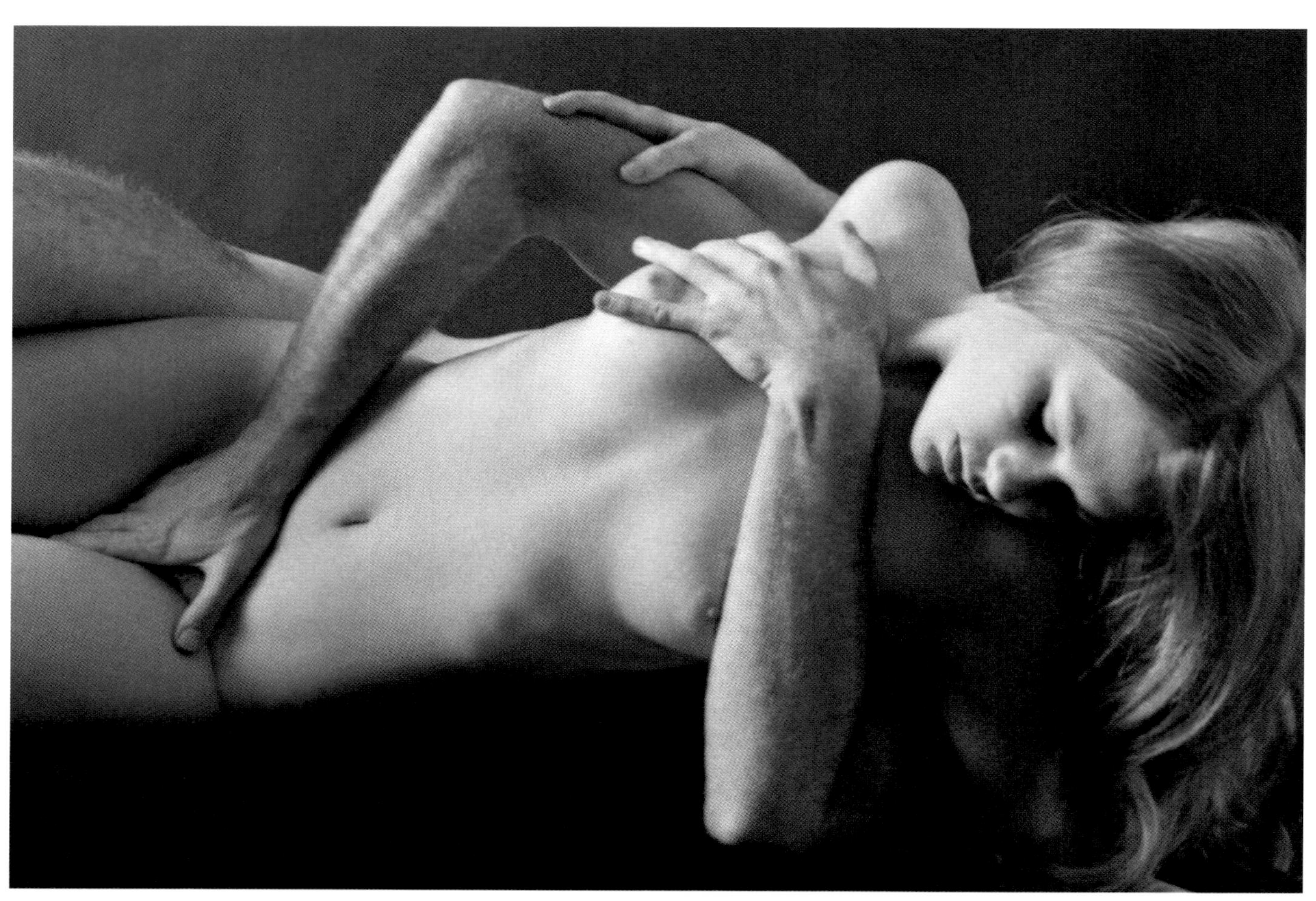

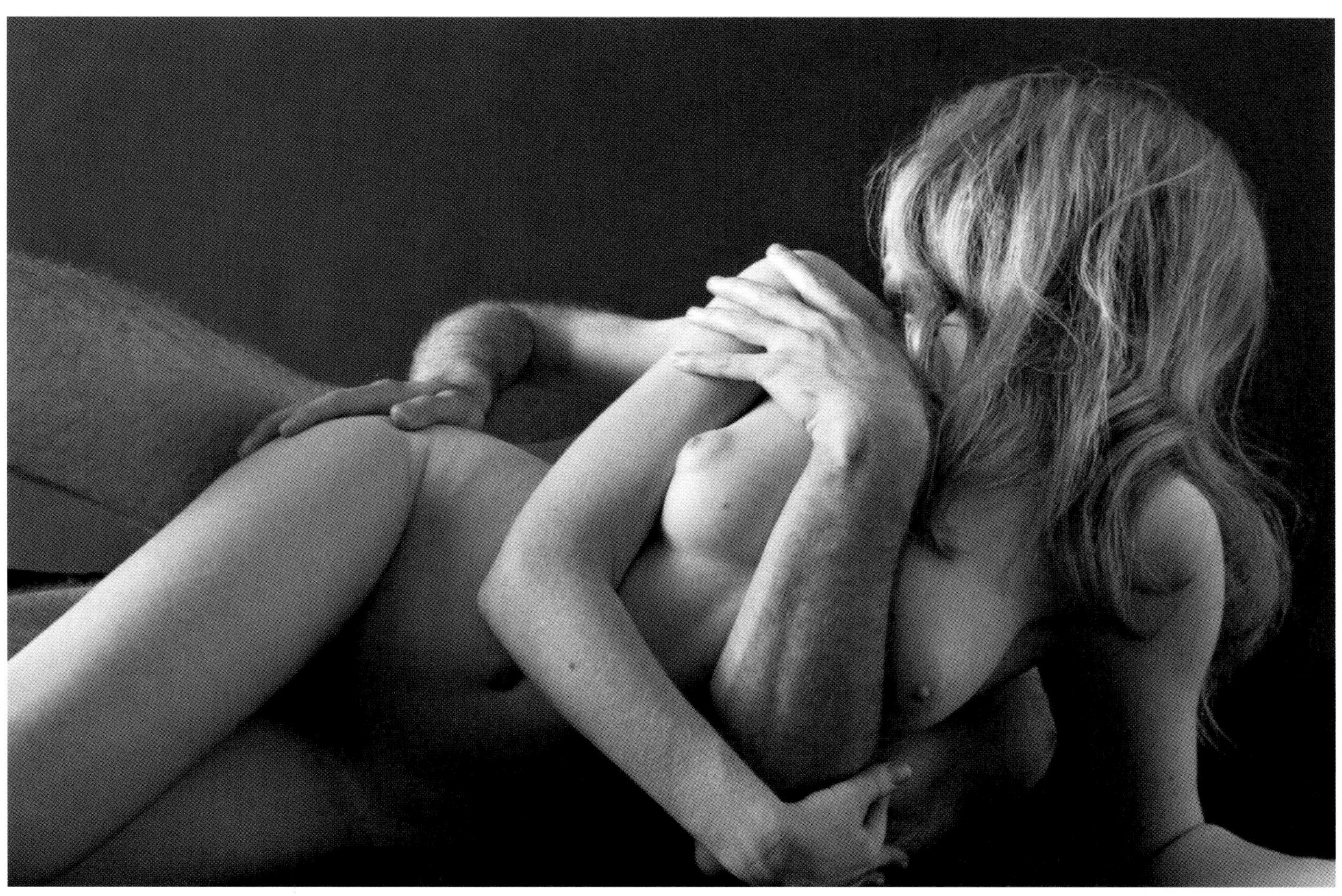

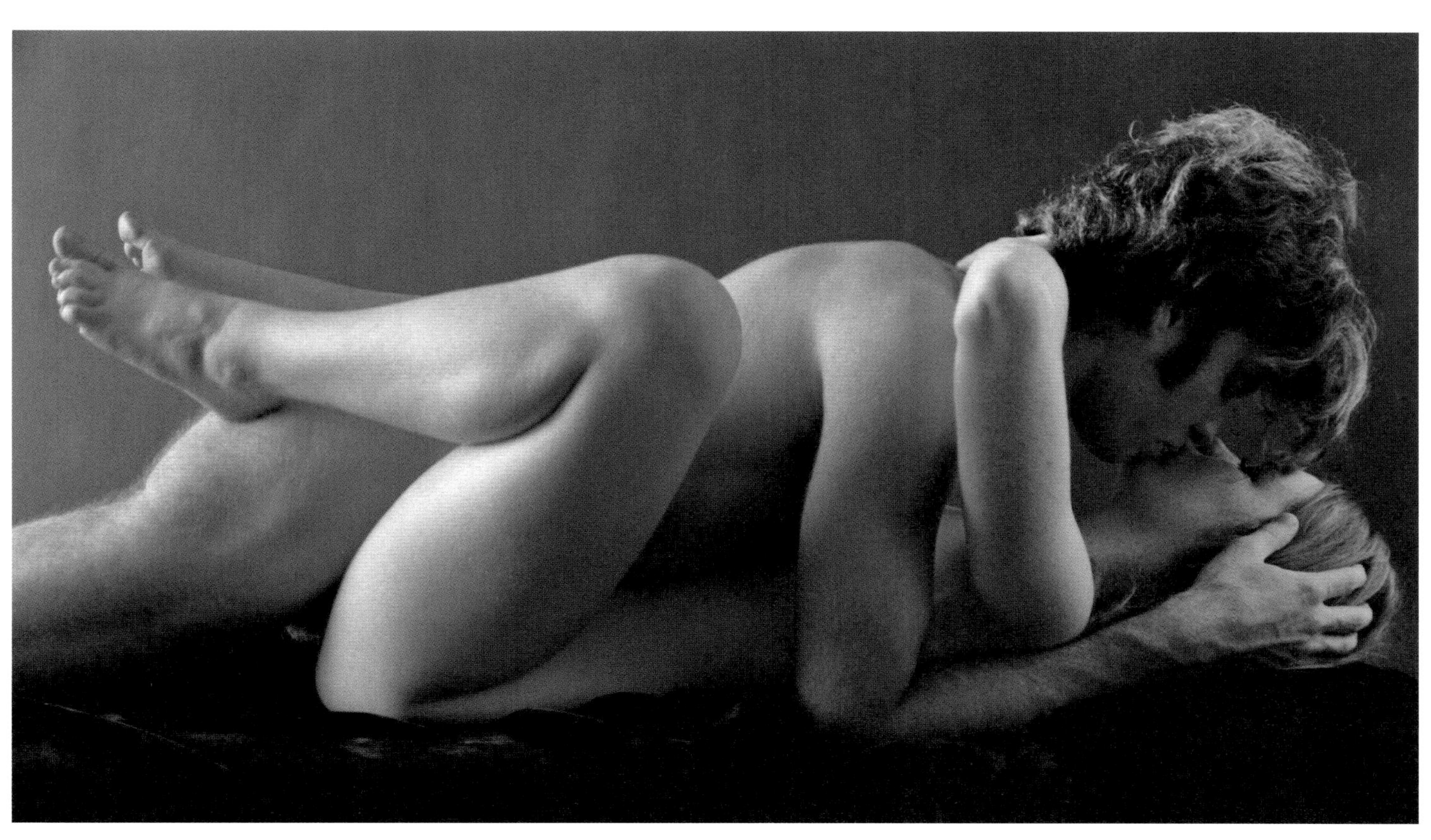

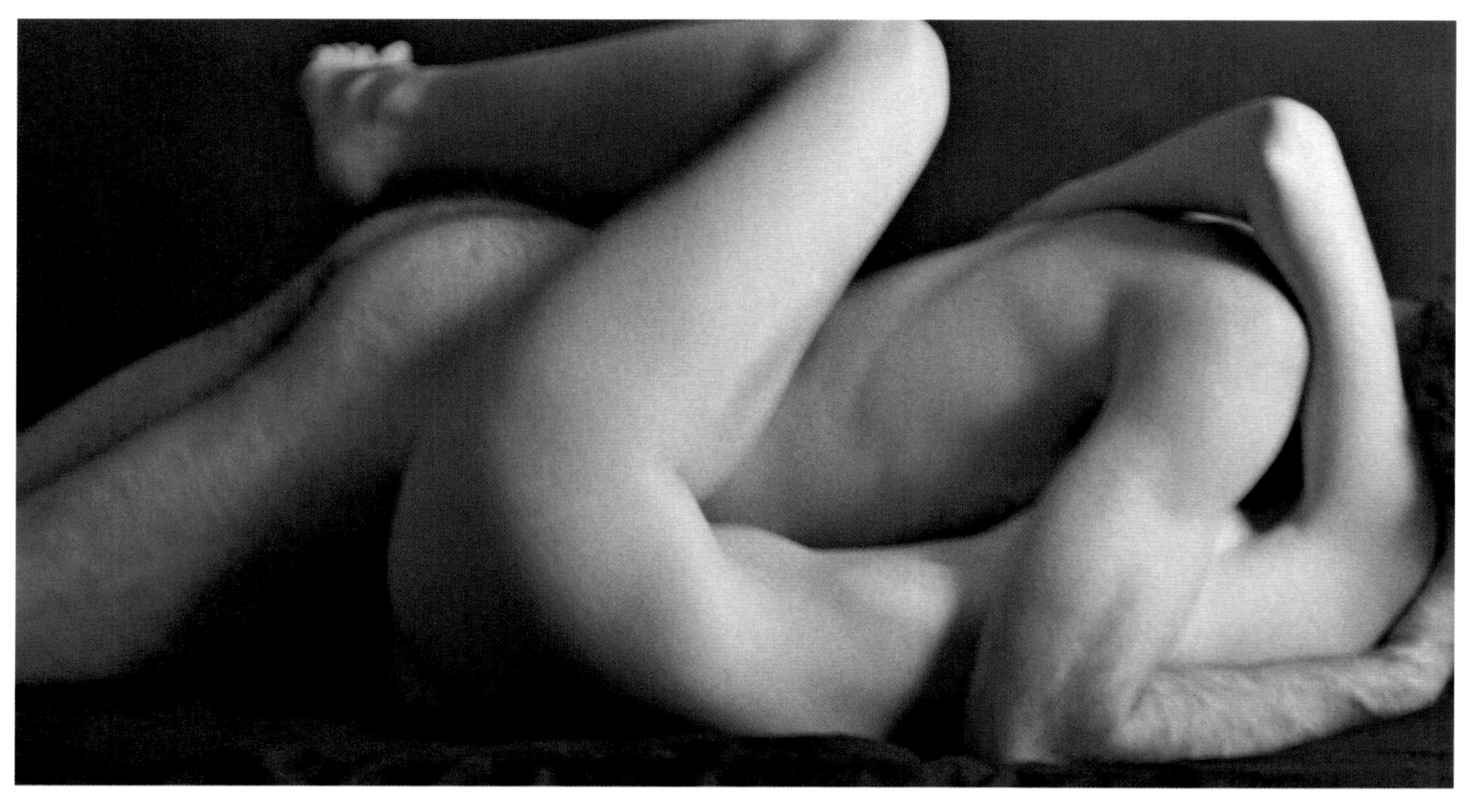

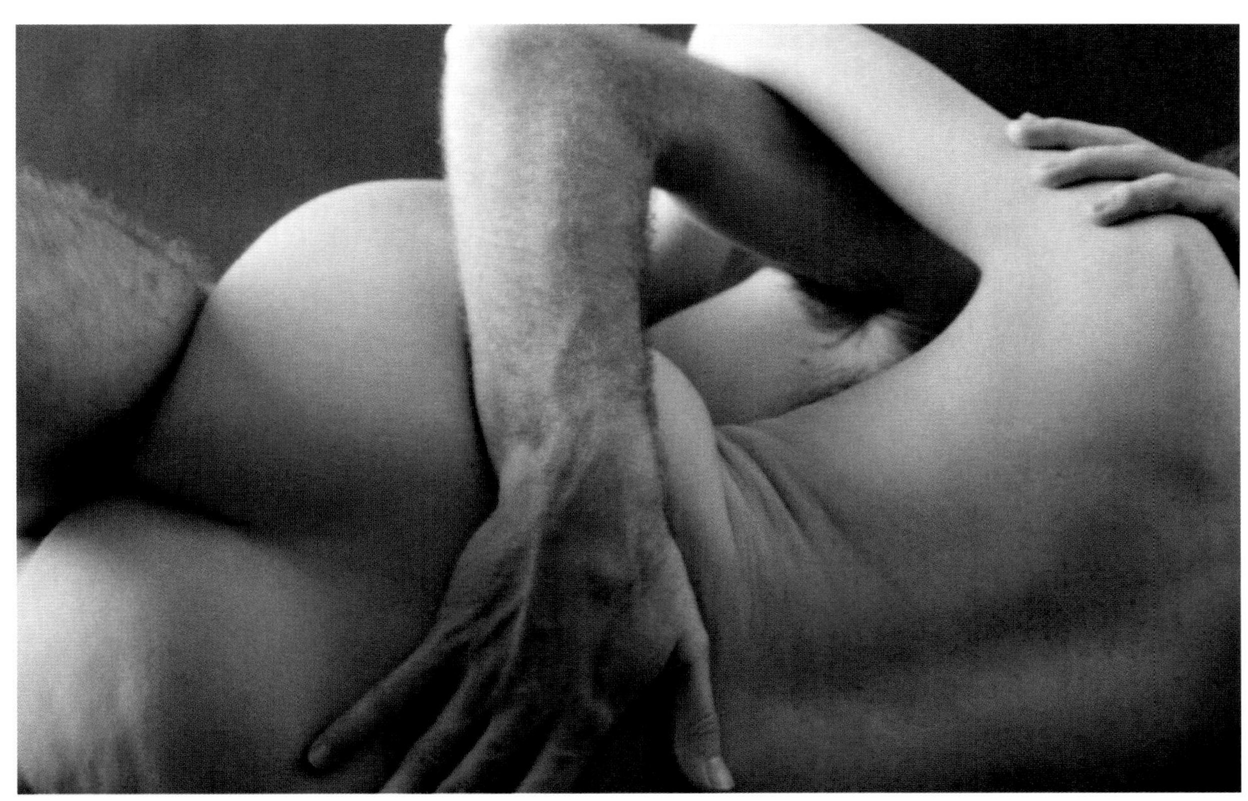

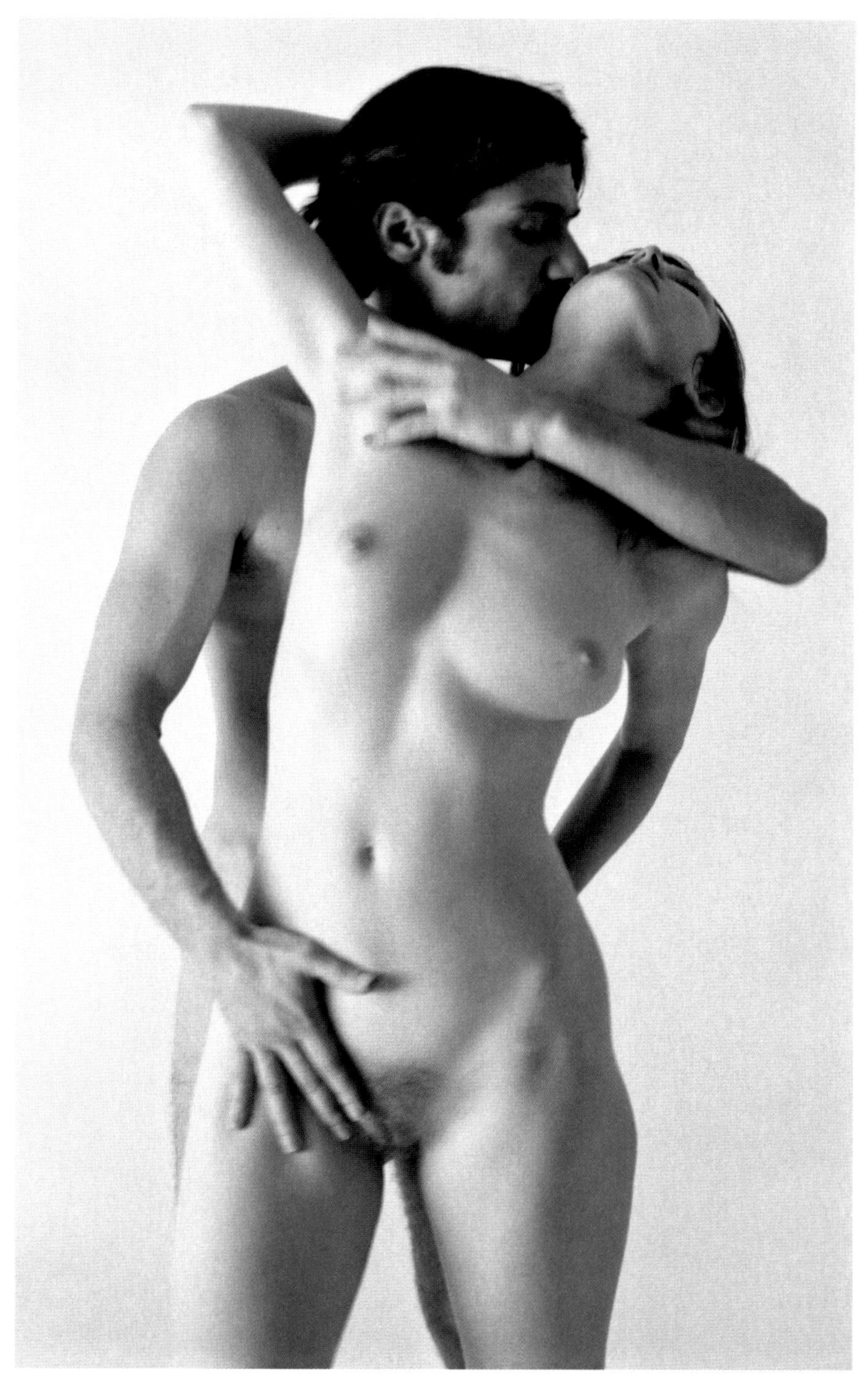

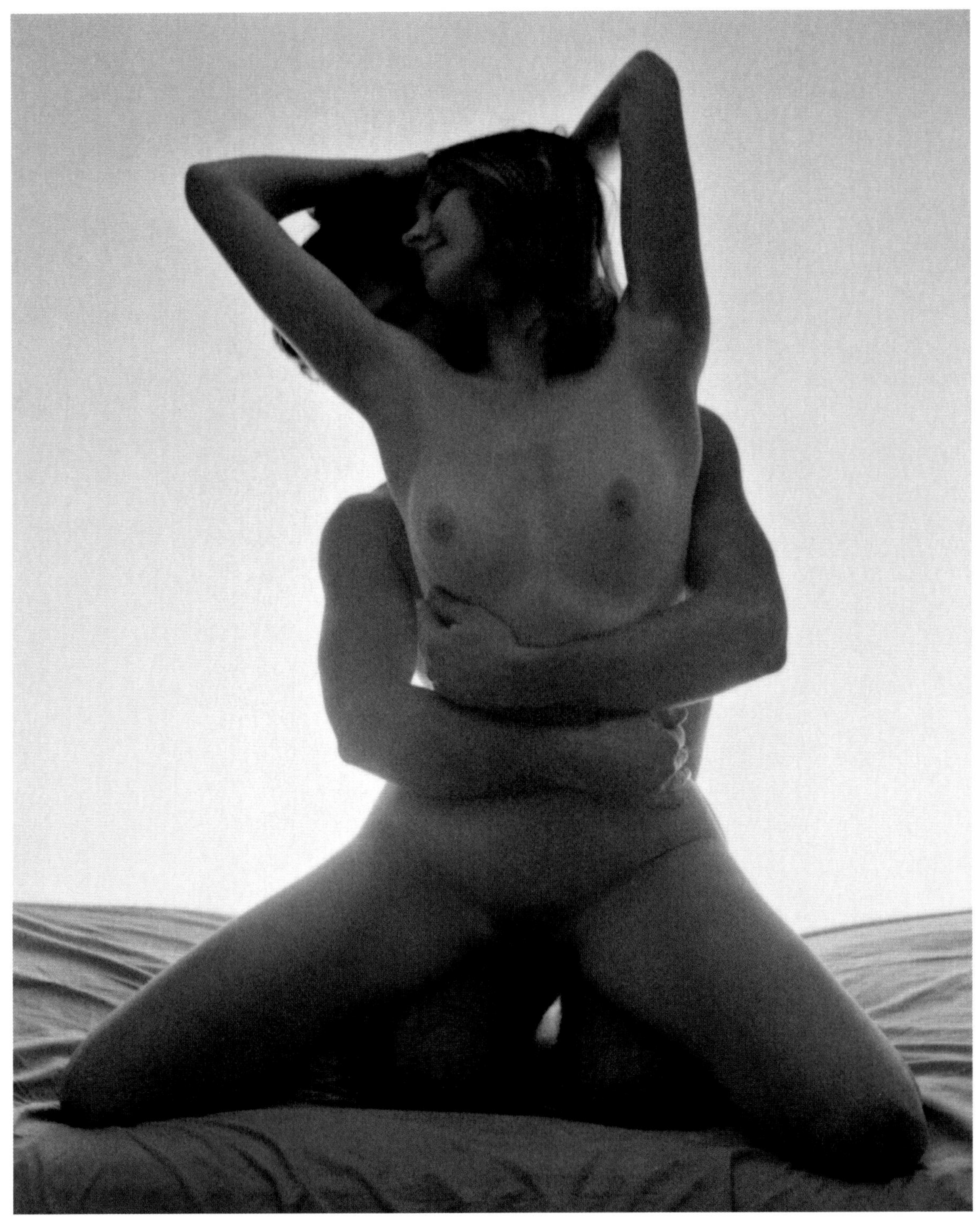

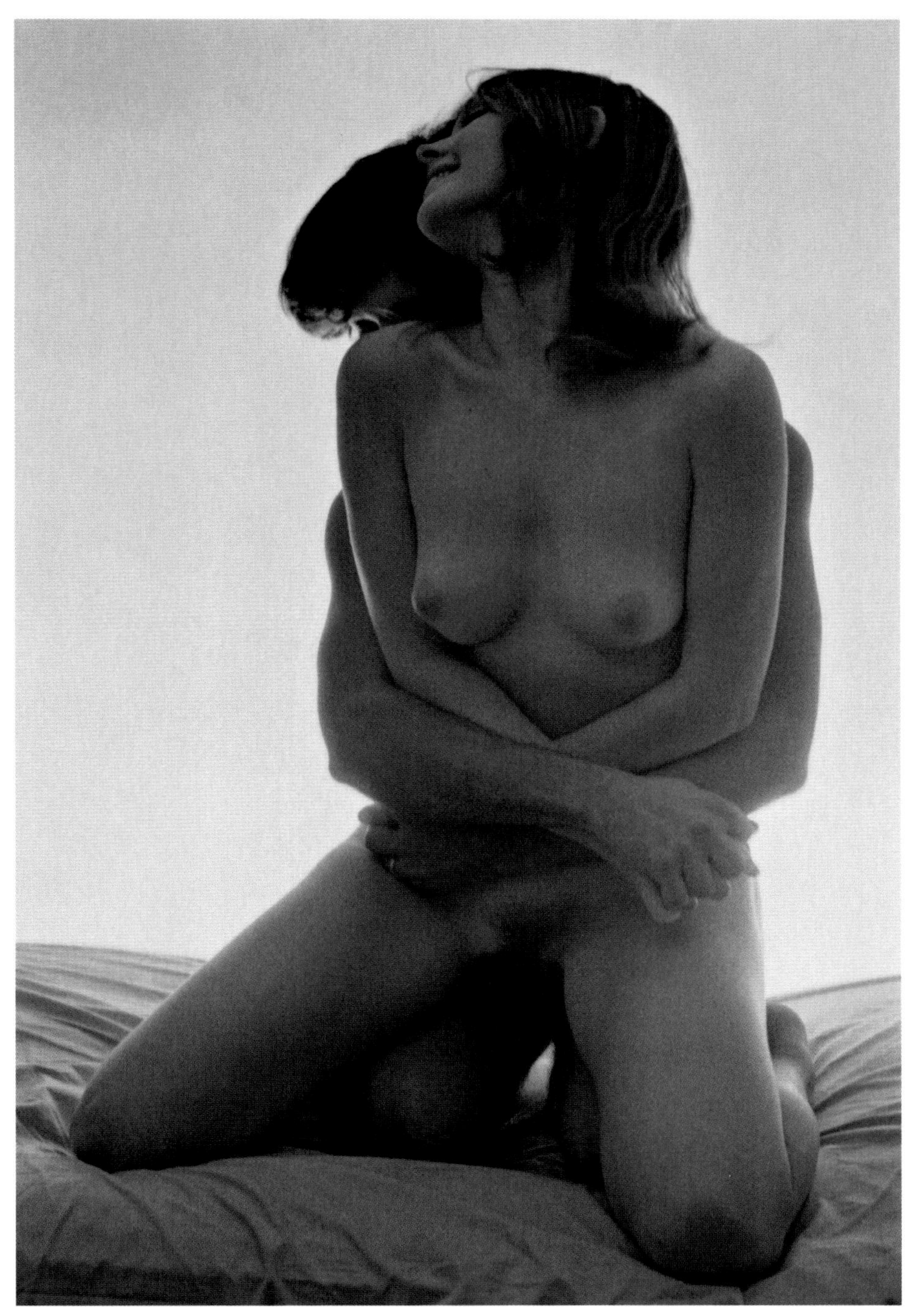

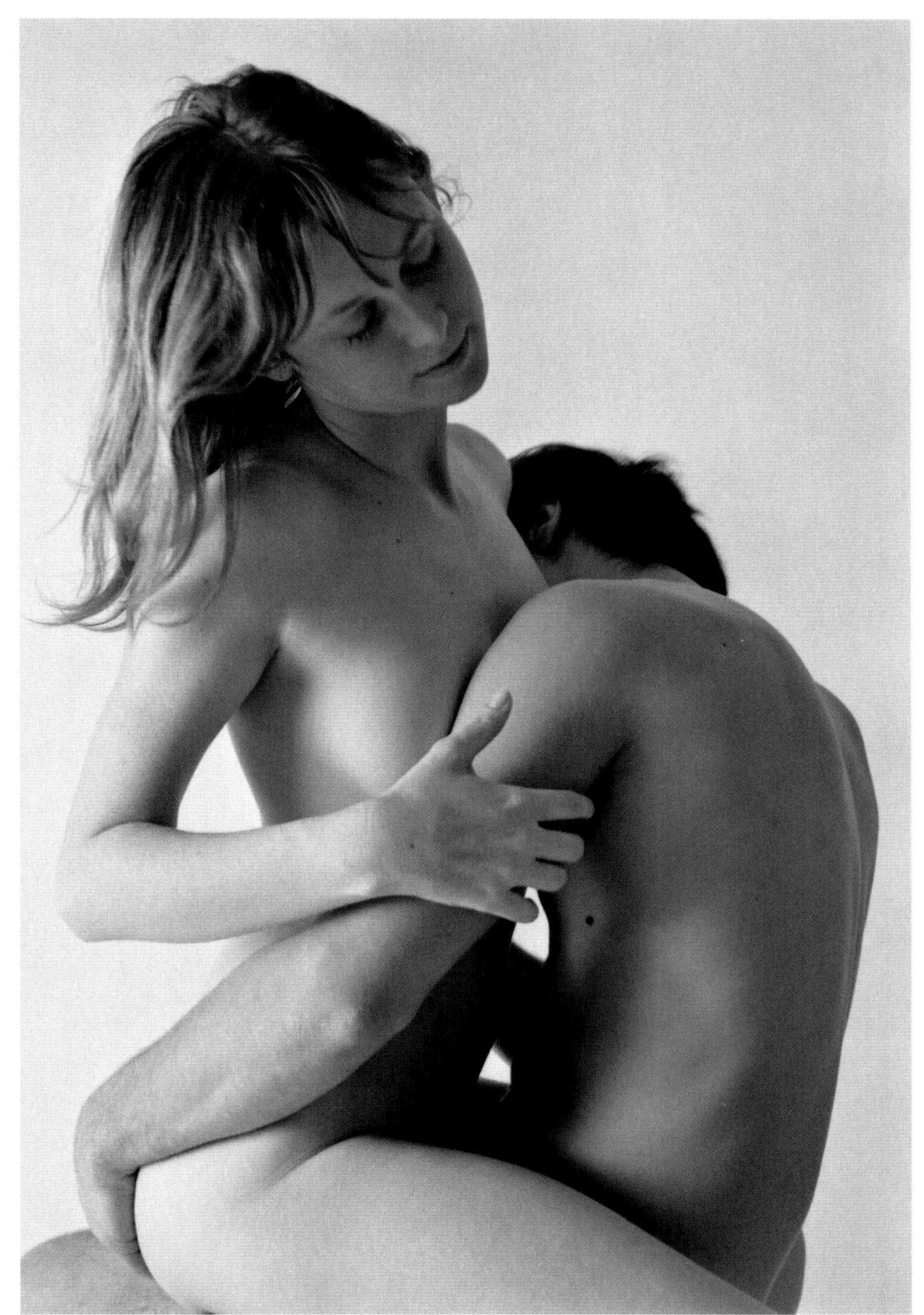

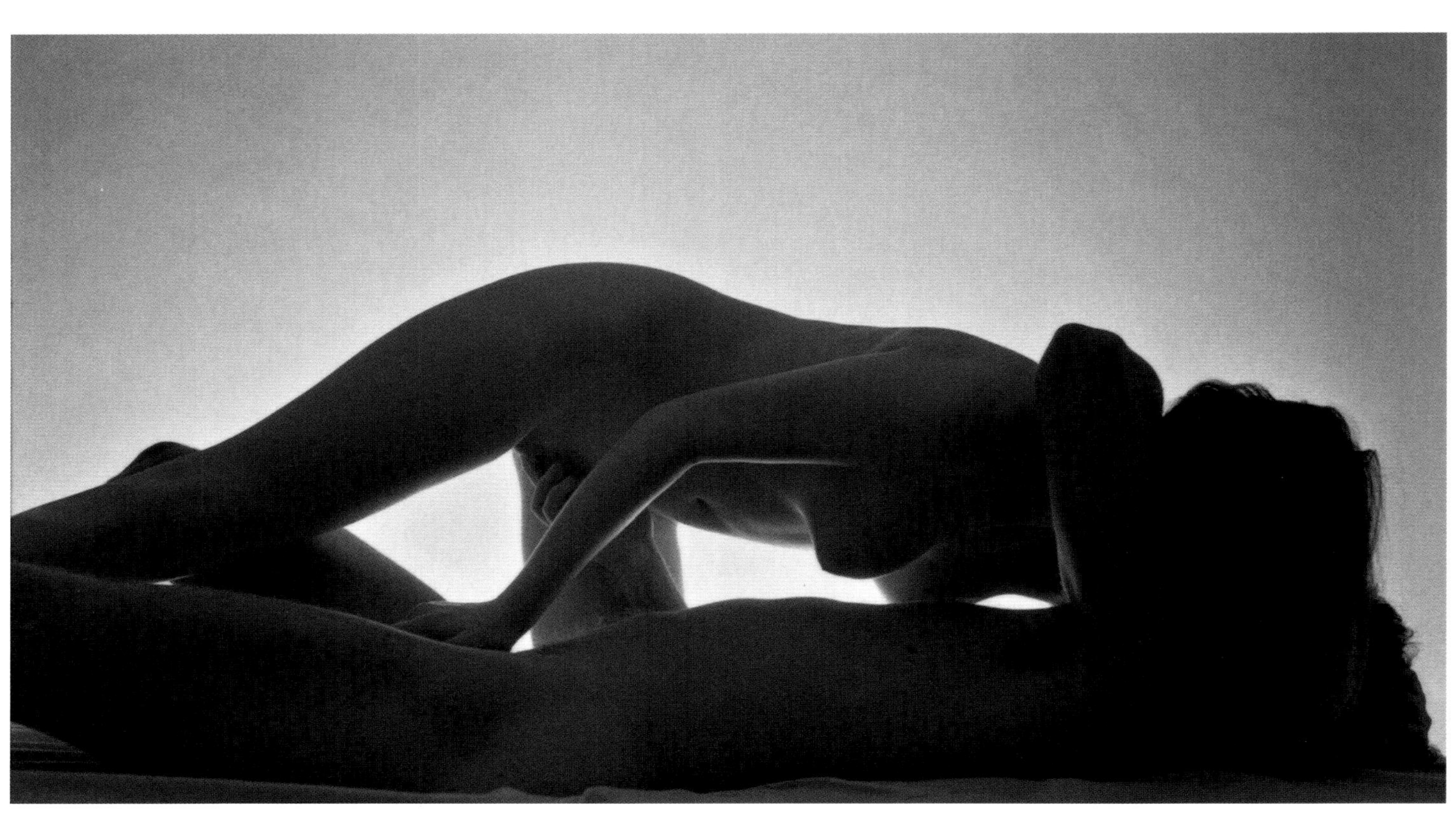

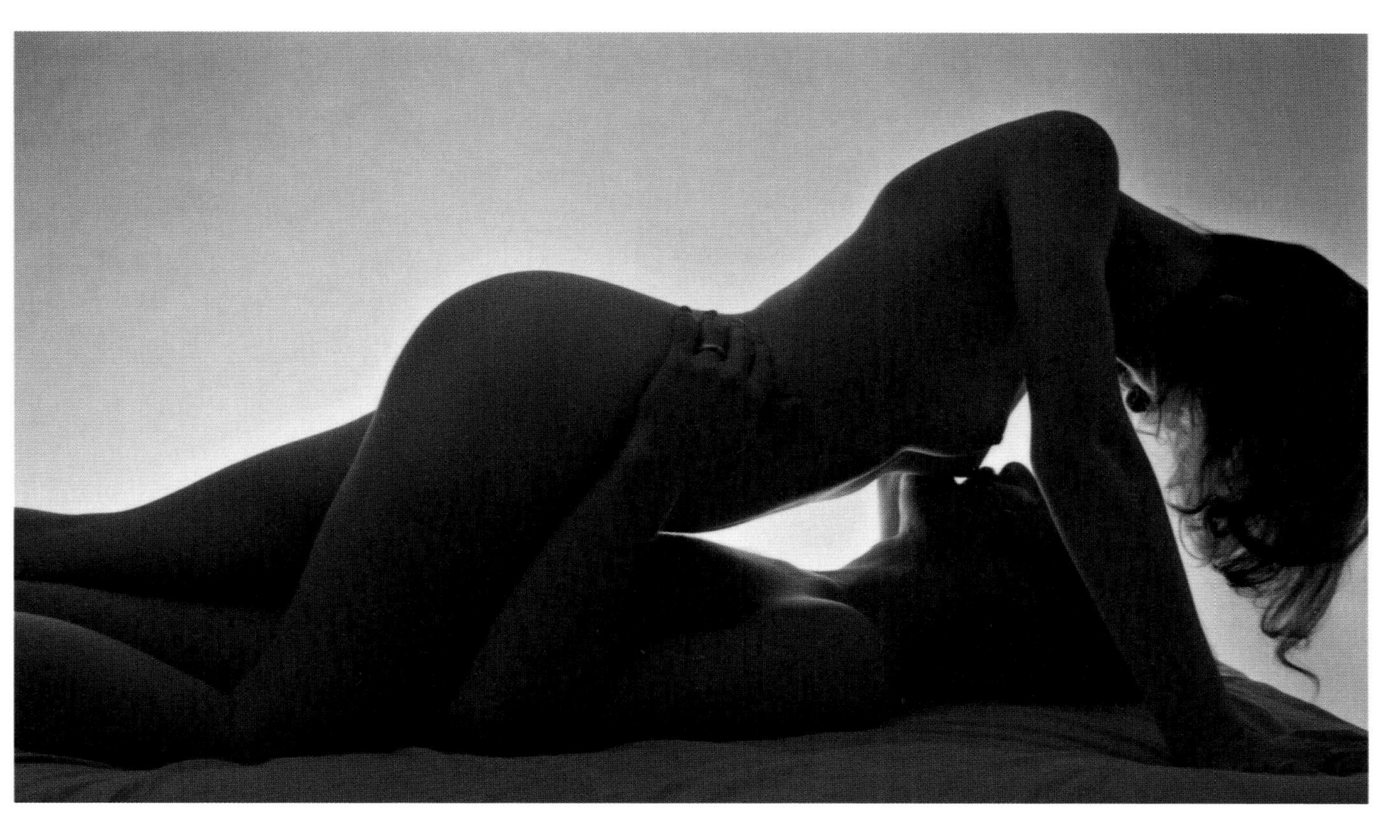

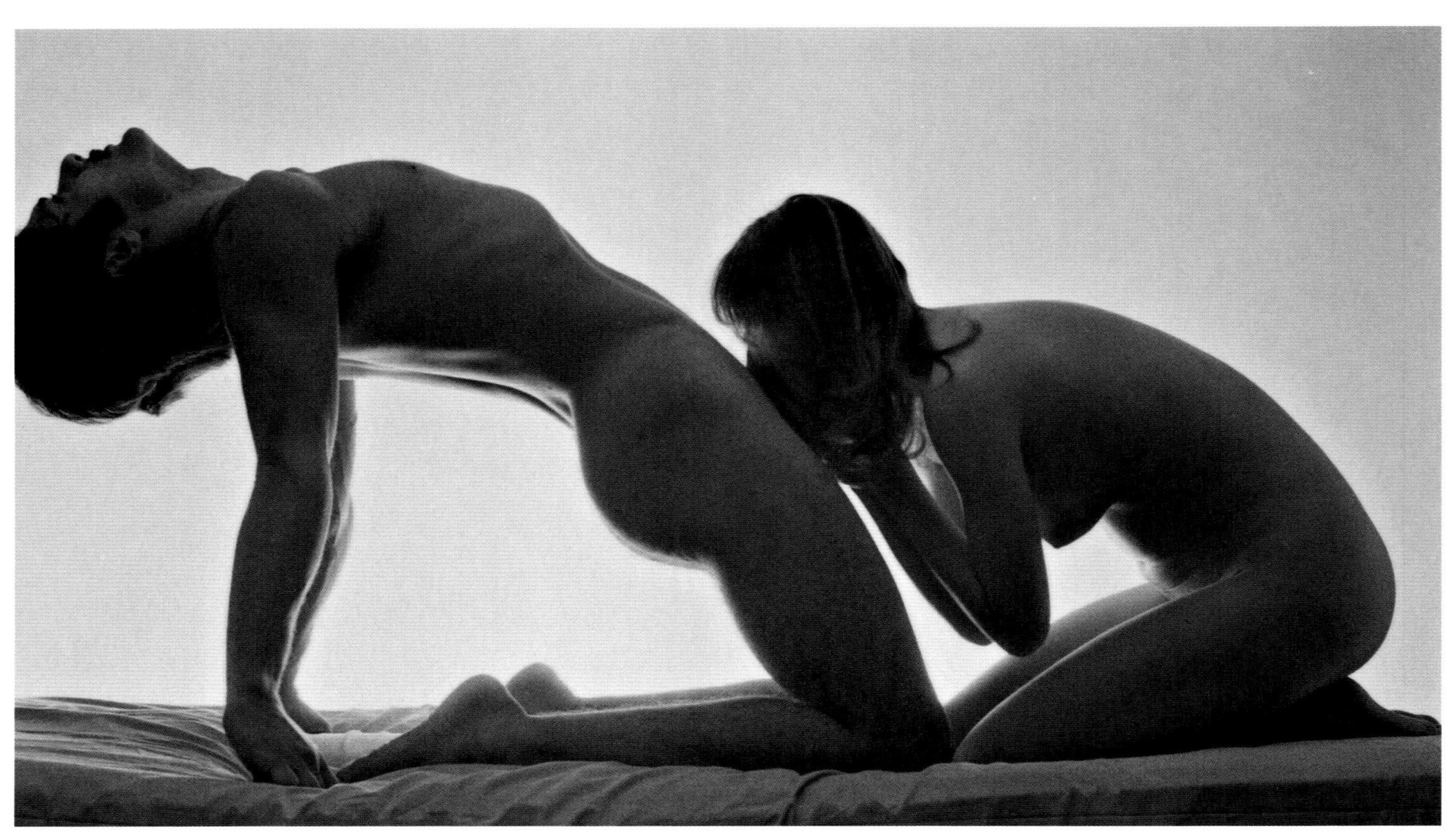

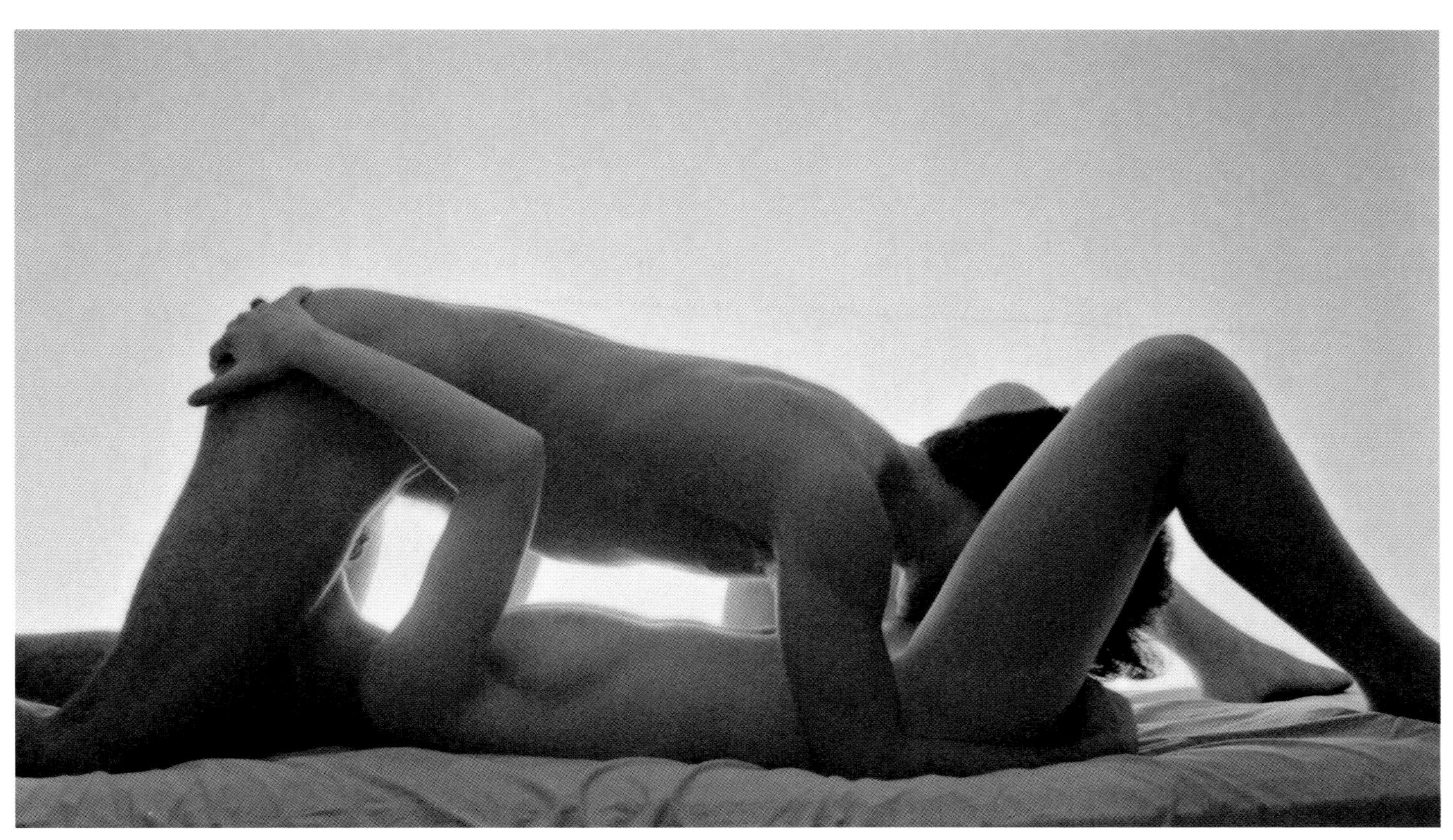

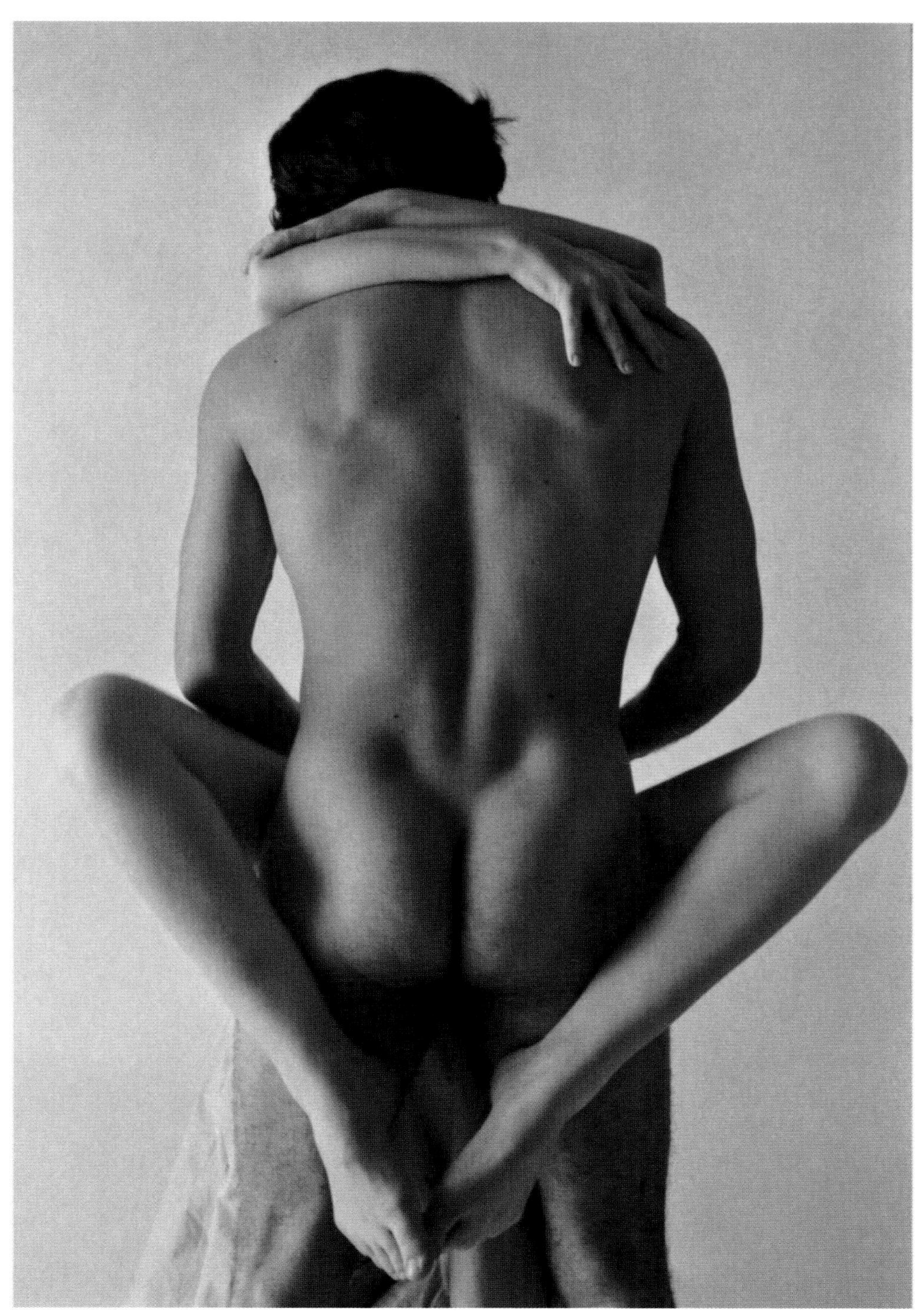

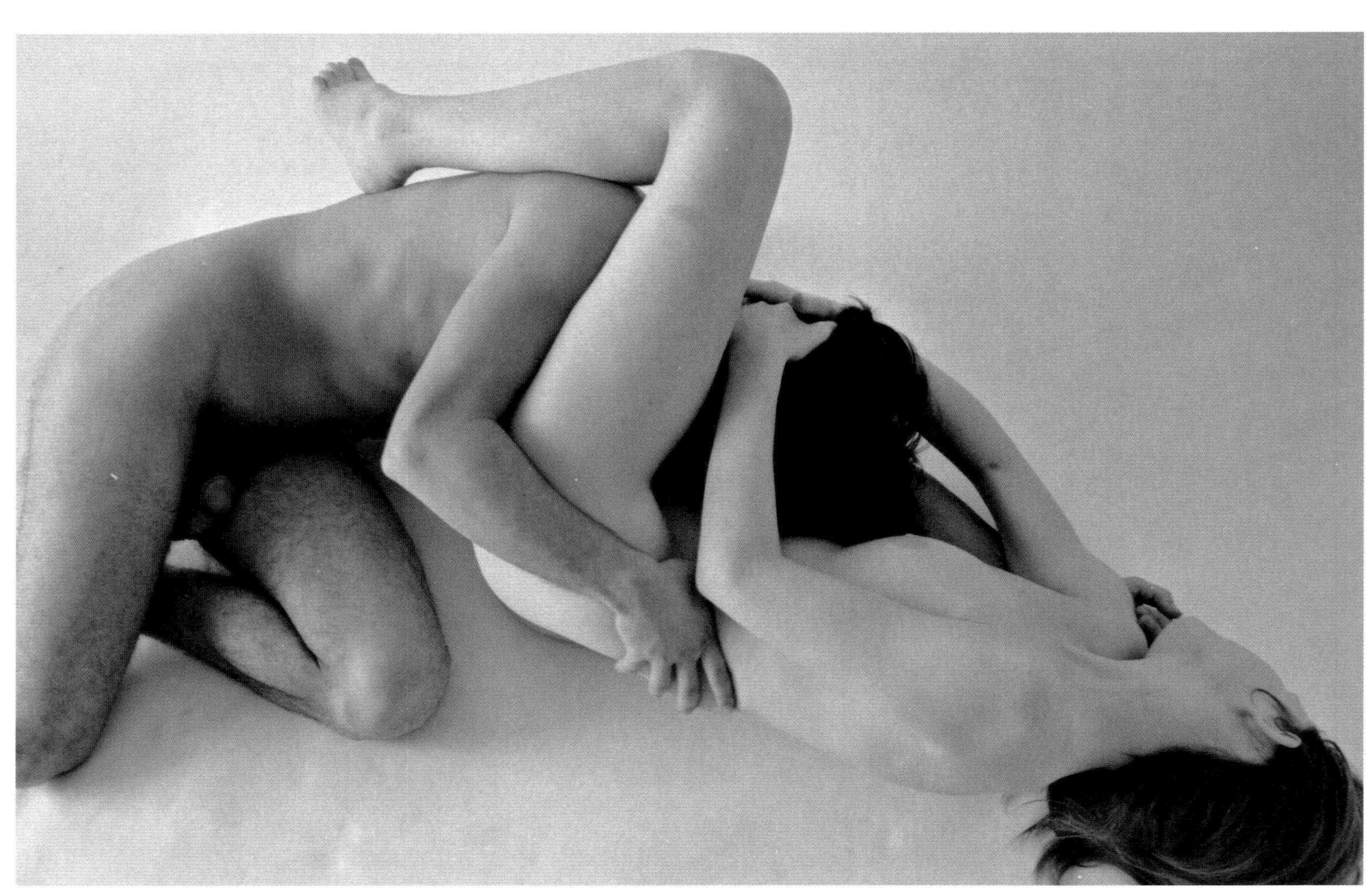

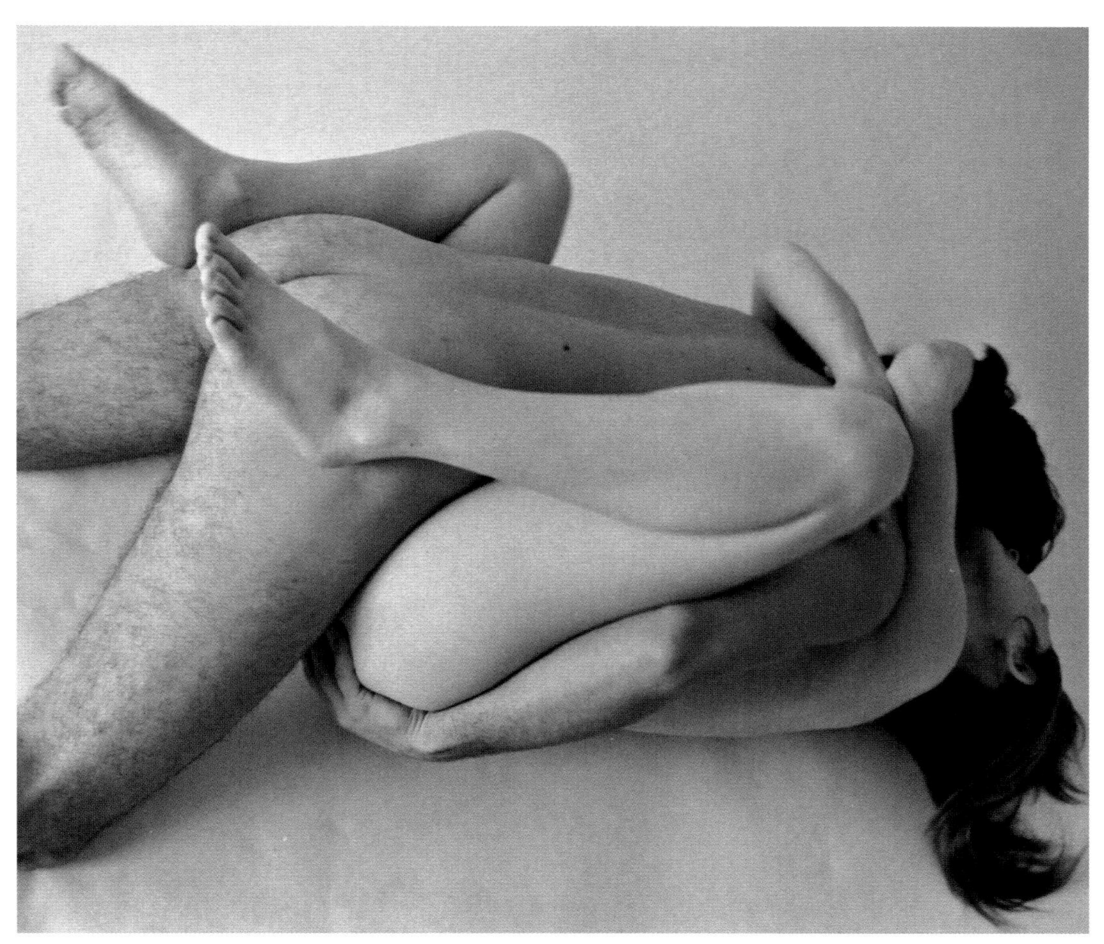

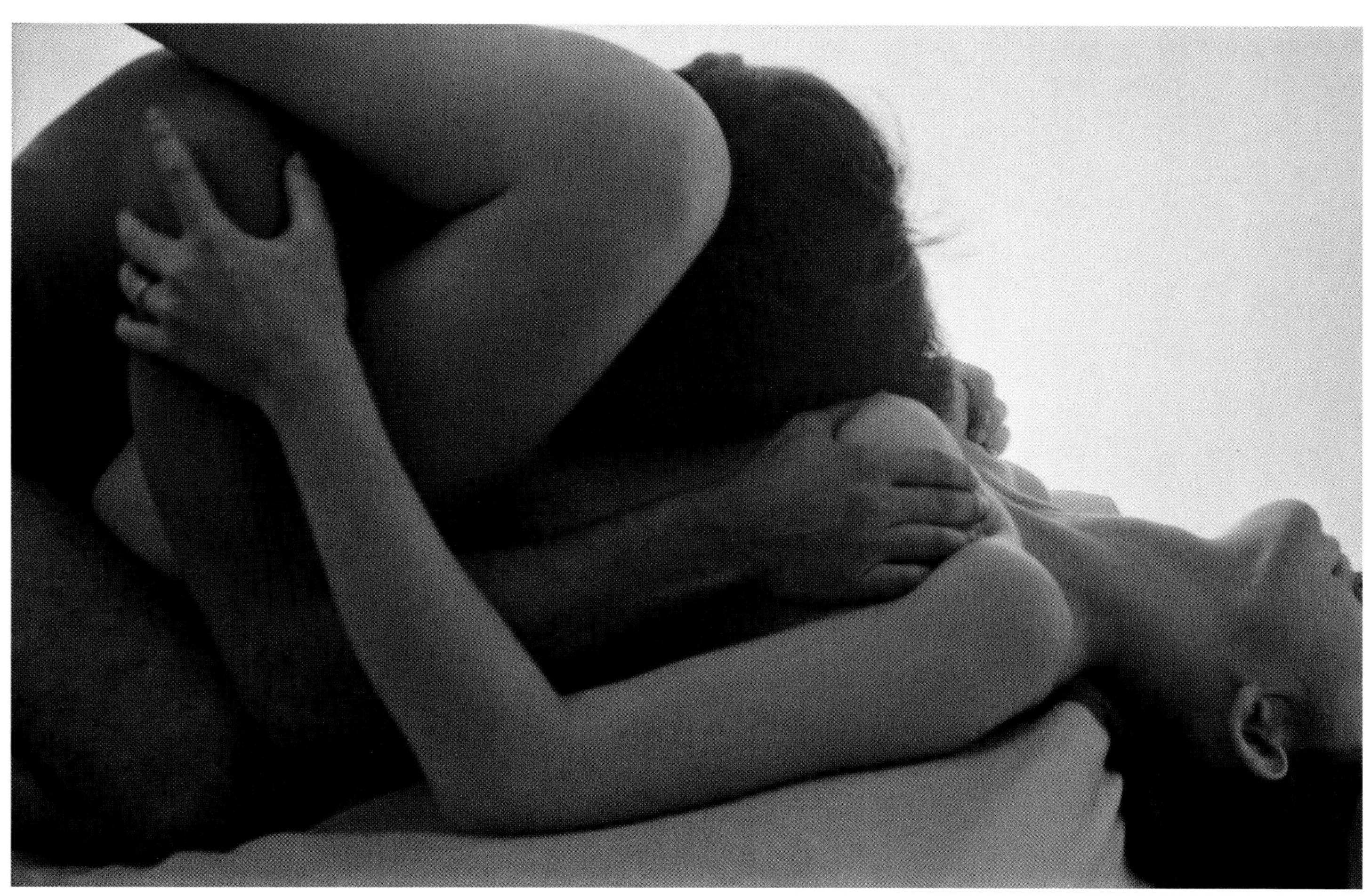

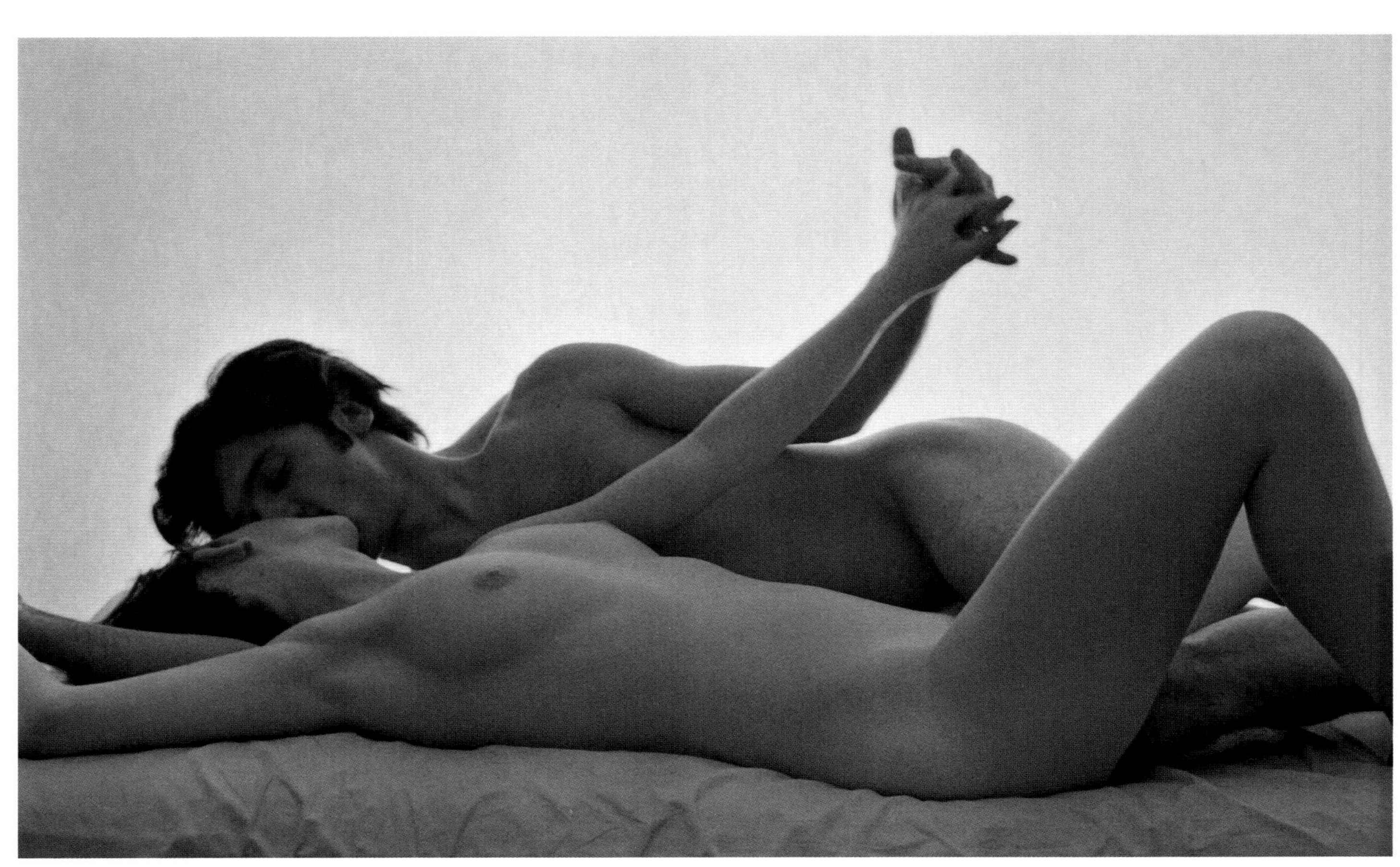

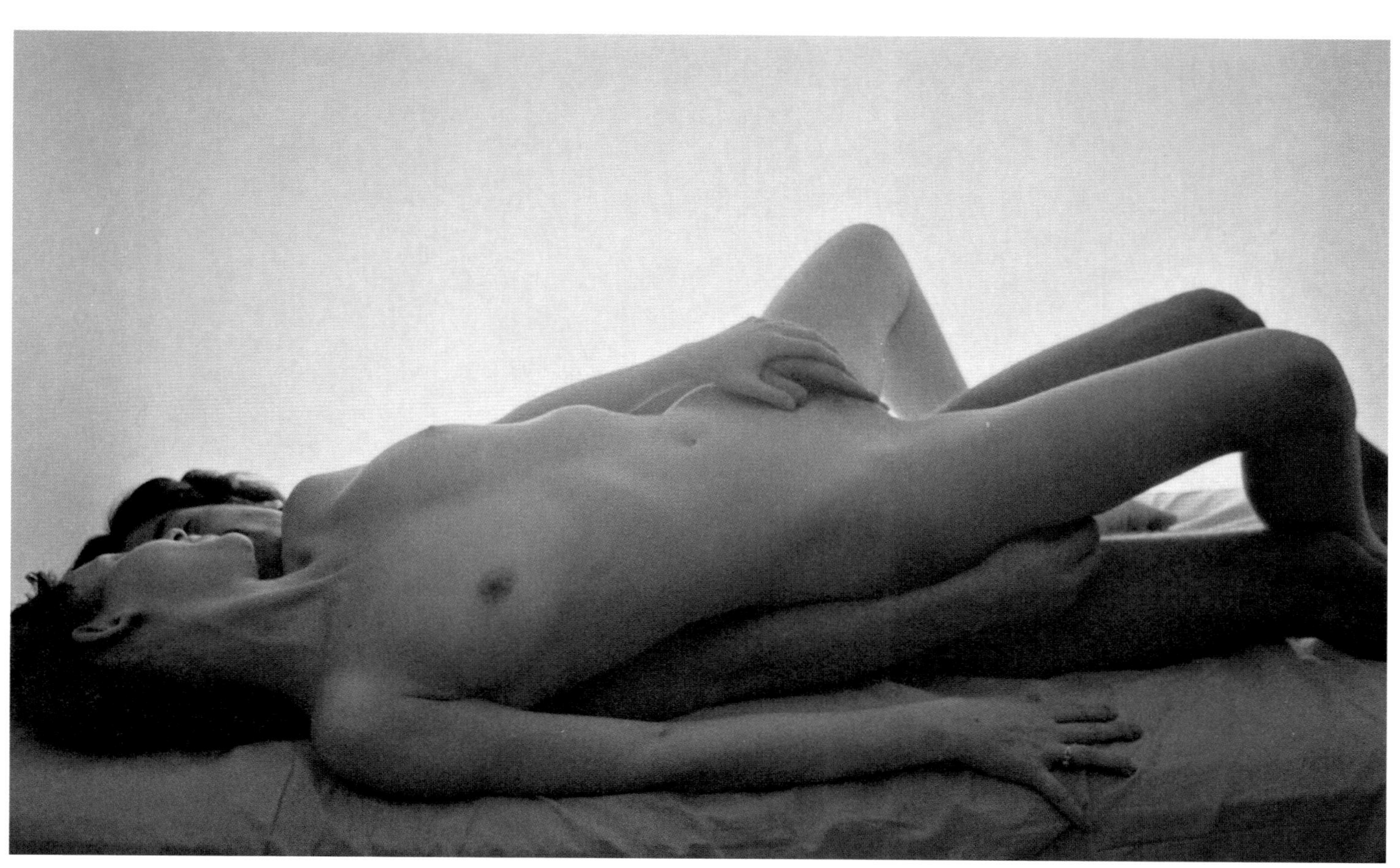

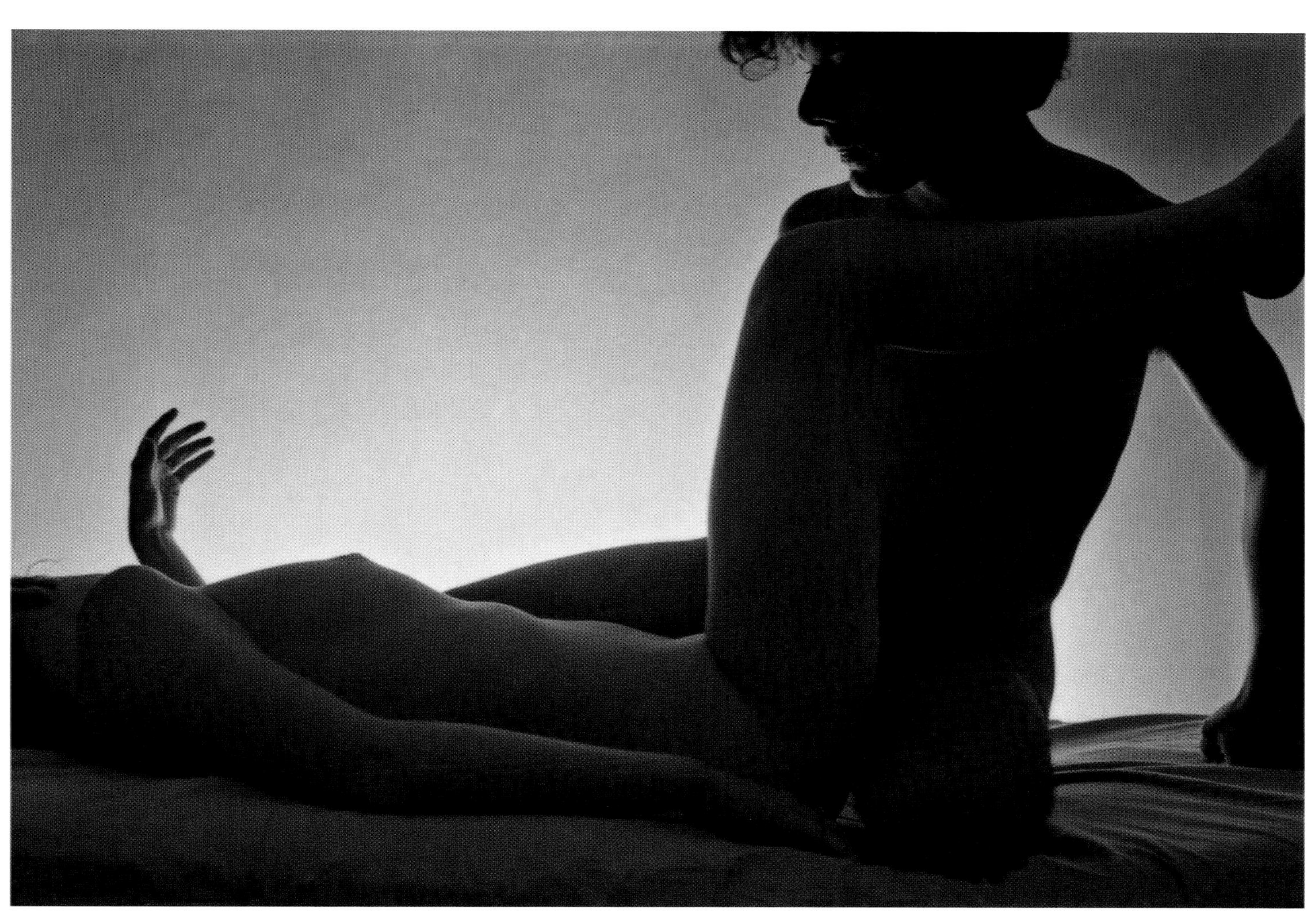

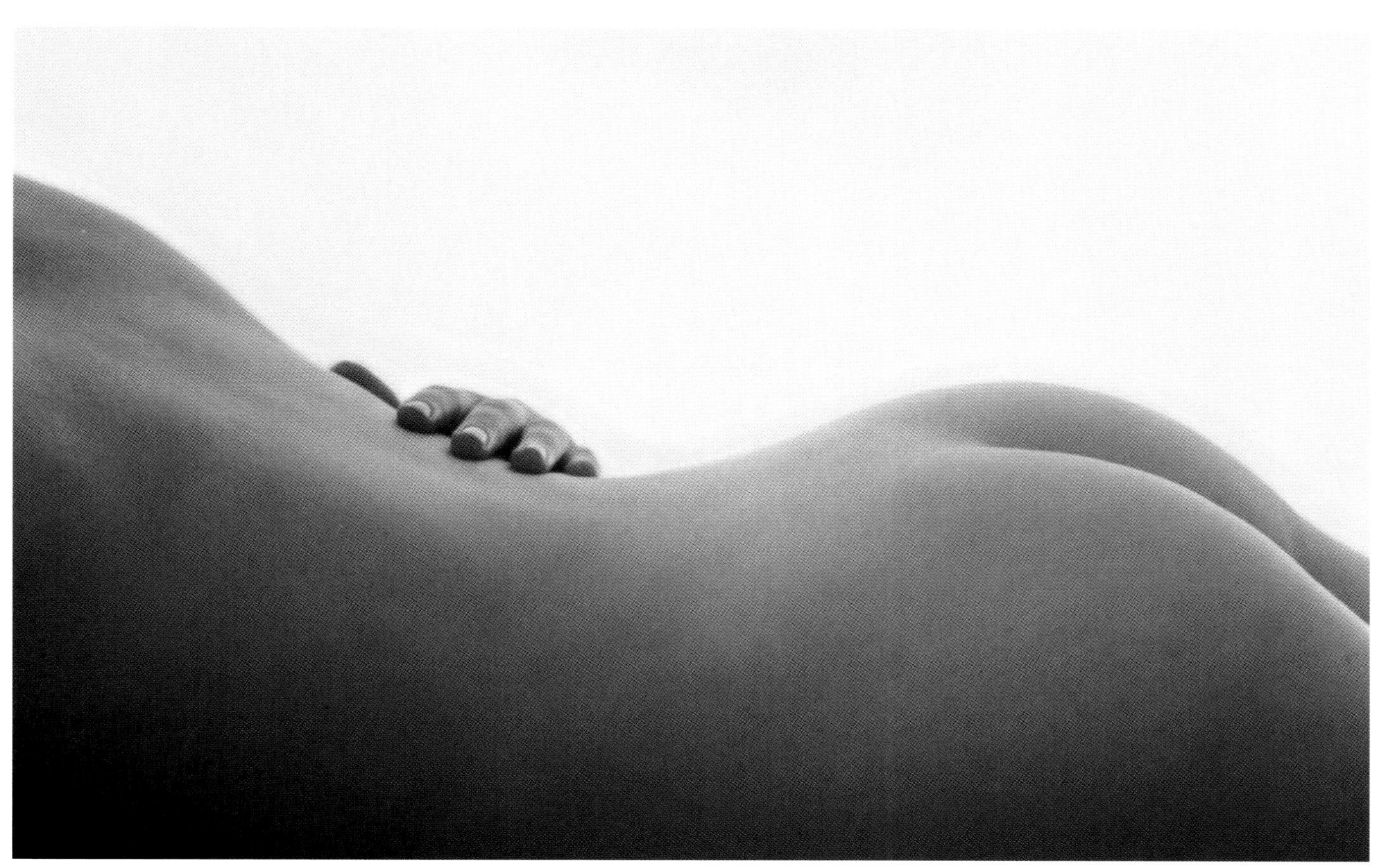